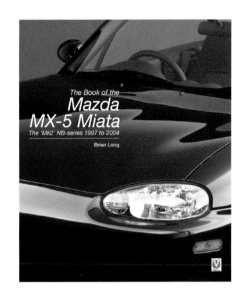

The Book of the
Mazda
MX-5 Miata
The 'Mk2' NB-series 1997 to 2004

Brian Long

Other great books from Veloce –

www.veloce.co.uk

First published in 1998 (*Mazda Miata Renaissance Sports Car*), and reprinted in 2000. Second Edition (*Mazda MX-5 – The Full Story of the World's Favourite Sportscar*) published in 2002. Enlarged, updated and redesigned Third Edition first published in October 2006, reprinted in October 2008 by Veloce Publishing Limited, Veloce House, Parkway Farm Business Park, Middle Farm Way, Poundbury, Dorchester DT1 3AR, England. Telephone 01305 260068 / Fax 01305 268864 / e-mail info@veloce.co.uk / web www.veloce.co.uk or www.velocebooks.com

The Book of the
Mazda
MX-5 Miata
The 'Mk2' NB-series 1997 to 2004

Brian Long

Contents

INTRODUCTION & ACKNOWLEDGEMENTS

Introduction

Although I'd always had a soft spot for the first of the rotary-engined RX-7s, promoted so ably through the competition exploits of Tom Walkinshaw and Win Percy in the UK, and a whole host of racing drivers in the States, it wasn't until 1991 that I really sat up and took notice of the Mazda marque. That was the year I'd travelled to Le Mans with Simon Pickford, a great friend of mine, only to be disappointed that my beloved Jaguars had been beaten, but filled with respect for the green and orange machine that kept bombing away, keeping me awake most of the night with its glorious – if rather noisy – exhaust note.

By that time, of course, the Mazda MX-5 had taken the world by storm. Following its launch in 1989, journalists from all corners of the world simply ran out of superlatives – nothing on the sporting front had created such a strong impression since the first appearance of the Datsun 240Z. The Hiroshima concern had introduced its inexpensive convertible at just the right time, providing owners with all the fun of older machines without any of the hassle. As many contemporary commentators stated, Mazda had reinvented the sports car.

Before long, the MX-5 (also known as the Miata or Eunos Roadster depending on the market) had gained a reputation that was the envy of the motor industry. The team behind the two-seater was not prepared to rest on its laurels, though, and brought out special versions and a whole series of stunning prototypes. By the end of 1997,

the best part of 450,000 examples had been built, and a mini-industry for aftermarket parts had grown up around the vehicle in virtually every country it was sold.

Smitten by the MX-5 himself, Rod Grainger of Veloce asked me if I'd do a book on the history of the car. I must say I had my doubts at the time. With a 1968 Alfa Romeo Spider Veloce sitting in the garage, the little Mazda had always seemed too contrived, and all too clinical to me. Anyway, I took the project on in the autumn of 1997, hoping in the back of my mind that if I did the MX-5 book first, maybe Rod would ask me to do a volume on the RX-7 later.

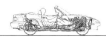

As it happens, my neutral attitude towards the project doubtless helped, for I was able to see the real enthusiasm behind the concept and how incredibly thorough Mazda had been, without falling into the trap of getting carried away by the myth and hysteria that seems to surround all cult cars, in much the same manner as rock and film stars. However, even from my standpoint, I didn't find many shortcomings, and grew to have a great deal of respect for the vehicle and the people behind it. After a few months of solid research, it was easy to see why the MX-5 had gained hordes of fans all over the world.

Meanwhile, between 1998 and 2006, *Mazda MX-5 Miata: The Book Of The World's Favourite Sportscar,* went to three editions with Veloce, each larger than its immediate predecessor due to the rapid evolution of the little two-seater, and I also became involved in a couple of other MX-5 titles in Japan along the way, too. For several years on and off, Rod and I have been trying to figure out how to go about keeping the Veloce book in print, as all the remaining copies were sold some time ago.

Unfortunately, for us to update the original Veloce title once more, would make it not only very heavy and expensive, but would also mean keeping some of the rare, attractive pictures from the early years quite small. We had no option as things were, trying to fit in the development story and production history of three distinctive vehicles into a reasonably sized and priced package. By splitting each generation into a separate volume, we can now do the illustrations justice, as well as add a few extra snippets of information along the way, as space is no longer an overwhelming concern.

The first volume – covering the original NA-series models – was released in 2015, and now we have this one on the next generation cars, which carried the NB moniker. Hopefully, we can do a book on the NC-series vehicles in the near future, as they, too, have picked up a strong following along the way, and we really need to bring that story up-to-date now we have the ND cars on the market. Anyway, in the meantime, I sincerely hope you will enjoy this new offering, which has a fair bit of new material in it, thanks to the space we have gained …

Acknowledgements

Reading through the original list of acknowledgements brought back a lot of memories. My wife, Miho, was the first person mentioned, which is only right given the amount of effort she put in translating Japanese documents for days on end. Her input really helped put things in perspective, although it's fair to say she's happier watching me translating German documents nowadays, as my recent workload has increasingly taken me back towards European cars.

In Japan, the first chap that came to my aid was Tamotsu Maeda, who was stationed in the PR department at the time, although he was very much a hands-on engineer in his day. I met him at the Tokyo Show the other day, and I'm pleased to report that he's still the same larger-than-life character he always was. Kensaku Terasaki was also involved, along with the lovely Mayumi Handa, who had a barrage of faxes from me back then, but never complained, and co-ordinated interviews with various development team members, including one with Shunji Tanaka, who went to Kawasaki soon after. Ryota Ogawa took over from Han-chan, helping me no end with the RX-7 book (that I did manage to do after all), and Kenichi Sagara came to my aid on many occasions before his services were snapped up by Volvo. The lady looking after me nowadays is Naoko Fujisaki, who works from Mazda's Tokyo office.

Special mention should be made of a few others, too. Takaharu Kobayakawa is an extraordinary man, and it is with great pride that I'm able to call him a friend. His weight opened a lot of doors at Mazda, for which I'm extremely grateful. Ironically, as the boss of that 1991 Le Mans campaign, after he retired from a lifelong career at Mazda, we went on to do the dealer training programme for Jaguar Japan together! As well as giving me a helping hand, Tom Matano wrote me a very special letter after the first book was published. It is something I shall treasure. Takao Kijima was also quick to react to my efforts, and it was wonderful to be able to include a Foreword by this engineering genius in the original titles. Although he has become a university lecturer now, I'm happy to say we've managed to stay in touch. Masanori Mizuochi was also very kind, filling in gaps on the M2 story, along with Hirotaka Tachibana, who has taken up a career in journalism after retiring from Mazda. I was also very lucky to have Shigenori Fukuda go over the text in his spare time, confirming and correcting statements with a level of enthusiasm displayed by all these legendary figures in MX-5 lore.

In America, Brian Betz, Ellen Clark, Jim Bright and Jennifer Newton came to the rescue, while Takahiro Tokura of Mazdaspeed, the folks at Mazda UK, and Bill Livingstone and Alan Beasley of IAD also pitched in. A ton of tuning companies and aftermarket suppliers also provided material, adding some breadth to the subject matter. Behind the scenes, too, people like Kenichi Kobayashi of Miki Press, Kenji Kikuchi of Nigensha, Michitake Isobe and Sachiko 'Miko' Miyoshi helped out in Japan, while Peter Hunter, Ian Robertson of Coventry Mazda and Paul Grogan of the MX-5 Owners' Club did their bit, providing and checking historical material for me. As with most of my books, this was a team effort, although few projects have relied on such on a big team as this one. Thank you, one and all …

Brian Long
Chiba, Japan

Chapter 1

A BRIEF HISTORY OF MAZDA

The history of the Japanese motor industry is a complex one, moulded and shaped by government decisions taken in the early 1930s and the reconstruction of Japan following the Second World War.

Mazda's origins date back to January 1920, with the founding of the Toyo Cork Kogyo Company Ltd by Jujiro Matsuda. As the name suggests, the Hiroshima-based firm initially concerned itself with cork products, but in the following year, Matsuda decided to move into the manufacture of machinery.

Matsuda was born in August 1875, and, despite being brought up in the fishing trade, developed an early interest in metalworking. By the age of 19 he had his own business; sadly, destined to fail. After various other enterprises, Matsuda eventually decided to move into the supply of cork, as the First World War stopped exports from Europe and left Japan in short supply. When Europe started exporting again, Matsuda guided the company back into light industry.

The car was still not a popular means of transport for the Japanese at that time. In the early 1920s, there were still fewer than 15,000 vehicles in the country, so automobile production was not considered commercially viable. However, a few two-wheeled machines were built following the devastating Kanto earthquake of 1923.

That year brought a flurry of imported trucks and buses from the United States to get the country mobile again. Most of Japan's population was centred around

Tsuneji Matsuda – the son of company founder Jujiro Matsuda, and the man responsible for guiding the Mazda brand in the post-war years.

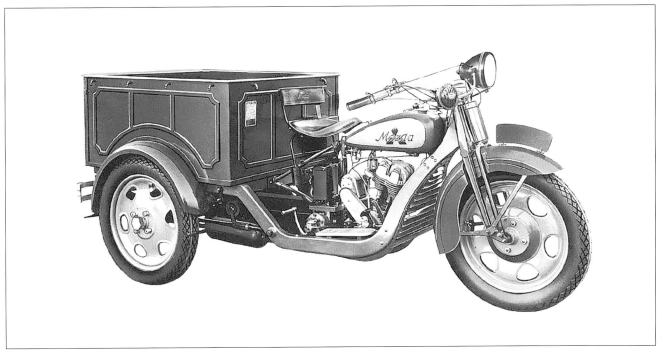

An early Mazda three-wheeler, with the diamonds on the fuel tank being there because the vehicles were distributed by the Mitsubishi Corporation until 1936. The company returned to the production of three-wheeler commercials following the end of the war, albeit of a more accomplished design with covered cabs as the 1950s progressed.

the Tokyo Bay (Kanto) area, and the earthquake had totally destroyed thousands of buildings, and most of the communications in Tokyo and Yokohama. Matsuda's Hiroshima-based concern, on the other side of the country, was not affected, and did its best to ease transport problems by building small two-stroke motorcycles.

Although the firm still dealt in cork (this section of the business wasn't sold off until 1944), light industry became increasingly important. In line with this gradual shift in emphasis, in July 1927, the business was renamed the Toyo Kogyo Co Ltd, which roughly translates as the Orient Industry Company.

The Mazda marque

Production of Toyo machine tools began in 1929, but, by 1930, thoughts were already turning toward motor vehicles. Design work was initiated on a three-wheeled truck (the 482cc Mazda DA), which entered production in October 1931.

As an aside, there is an interesting story behind the choice of the Mazda name. In Persian mythology, the 'lord of light and wisdom' was called Ahura Mazdah. The Mazdah title sounded good in almost any language and had an ideal meaning, with the added bonus that the founder's family name was Matsuda (in Japanese, it sounds very similar to Mazdah). Subsequently, the letter 'h' was dropped and the Mazda marque was born.

The DA was a great success, and, within a few months of starting production, Toyo Kogyo began exporting the three-wheeled Mazda to Manchuria, an area of China occupied by Japan. Toyo Kogyo continued to develop the three-wheeler, giving it a larger engine, and also started to manufacture gauge blocks and machine drills.

The company's capital increased no fewer than four times during 1934, and the factory – based in the Fuchu area of Hiroshima – was duly enlarged. However, military considerations soon led the government to pass the 1936 Motorcar Manufacturing Enterprise Law. Although only Nissan, Toyota and Isuzu complied with the new law at the time, it effectively ended the activities of foreign car companies, with both Ford and General Motors initially cutting back production and then closing their factories in Japan during 1937.

Toyo Kogyo was forced to make munitions for the Army, although a few three-wheelers continued to leave the factory, despite the Enterprise Law. By 1940, Mazda had built a small prototype coupé, but before it could be developed further, production switched completely to armaments in the build-up to the Pacific War.

After the attack on Pearl Harbour, America declared war on Japan, but no-one could have foreseen the dreadful events that would follow. On 6 August 1945, Hiroshima became a scene of complete devastation. A broadcast from Tokyo Radio stated: "Most of Hiroshima

The first Mazda car was the R360 Coupé of mid-1960, powered by a tiny air-cooled V-twin. Over 20,000 examples were sold in the first year of production.

no longer exists. The impact of the bomb was so terrific that practically all living things, human and animal, were literally seared to death by the tremendous heat and pressure engendered by the blast." The Toyo Kogyo factory, partially sheltered by a hill, was just far enough away from the centre of the blast to escape heavy damage. Sadly, though, the bomb dropped by *Enola Gay* claimed 78,000 lives and injured countless others. The end of the Second World War came later that month, but it was many years before some kind of normality was restored to the lives of those – on both sides – who suffered as a result of the conflict.

Post-war growth
Although the factory was being used as a makeshift hospital and 'town hall,' Toyo Kogyo managed to resume production of the Mazda three-wheelers at the end of 1945. Three years later, the company's capital had doubled, and up to 200 vehicles were being built each week. Larger commercials were announced in 1950, but it was another decade before the company moved into the passenger car business.

Various laws were passed to help the Japanese motor industry, and gradually it found its feet. Production rose steadily, new roads were built, and Tokyo streets began to fill with Japanese cars rather than ageing imported models. Steel and components were being produced in Japan, as by now most of the factories had been returned to their previous owners by the Occupational Forces, thus reducing the need to buy from foreign countries.

Commercial vehicles continued to sustain the Hiroshima concern, but, in April 1960, the company introduced its first car – the R360 Coupé. It went on sale in May with an air-cooled, V-twin engine mounted at the rear; although the 356cc unit developed only 16bhp, the R360 could be bought with either a manual or automatic transmission and was capable of 56mph (90kph). It sold exceptionally well, with over 20,000 built in the first year.

After the war, a number of Japanese manufacturers had taken the opportunity to enter into technical co-operation agreements with companies in the west. The Toyo Kogyo concern was quite late in taking up this offer,

but eventually, in mid-1961, signed a deal with NSU of Germany.

NSU held the rights to the Wankel rotary engine, a rather advanced piece of engineering. It was felt that being the first vehicle builder in Japan to acquire this technology would enable Mazda to catch up with the likes of Nissan and Toyota, thus ensuring its survival.

Over the next five years, while the rotary engine was being developed, Toyo Kogyo introduced a number of new Mazda cars – the Carol P360 and P600, the first generation of Familia models, and the Luce 1500. (The coachwork on the latter was designed by a famous Italian styling house; in fact, Giugiaro has been credited with the design during his time with Bertone.)

Meanwhile, cumulative production of cars and commercials reached one million units in March 1963; two years later, the Miyoshi Proving Ground was completed. By this time, Toyo Kogyo was the third largest car producer in Japan, continually expanding operations at a staggering rate. In 1966, a new passenger car plant opened in Hiroshima, and, in the following year, full-scale exports for the European market began.

The rotary revolution

Toyo Kogyo – under the leadership of Jujiro Matsuda's son, Tsuneji, since 1951 – was certainly a forward-thinking organisation, installing its first computer system at Hiroshima as early as 1958. Six years later, at the 1964 Tokyo Show (held at Harumi that year), the Mazda Cosmo Sport 110S made its debut.

Powered by the company's first Wankel engine, it was extremely advanced, and gave the Rotary Engine Development Division more than a few teething problems in the early days. It underwent an extraordinary period of development before going on sale to the public, with a total of 60 pre-production models road tested. Consequently, the Mazda Cosmo did not go on sale until 30 May 1967, by which time the company's engineers

A 1969 advert for the rotary-engined Cosmo Sport 110S. Its high price tag limited total sales to just over 1500 units over a six-year production run.

An official photograph of the 1973 RX-4 Coupé from the UK concessionaires. The era known as the 'Sporting Forties' (1965 to 1974 expressed in terms of the reign of the Emperor) spawned a number of exciting vehicles from Japan.

Although not the most interesting Mazda ever built, the conventional Familia (known as the GLC in America and the 323 elsewhere) helped Toyo Kogyo survive an uncertain period in the company's history.

had perfected the power unit. Selling at 1,580,000 yen, it was very costly (only the Toyota 2000GT was more expensive in the sports car sector of the Japanese market), and this was reflected in a total run, from 1967 to 1972, of just 1519 units.

In October 1969, the Japan Automatic Transmission Company (JATCO) was formed: a joint venture between Toyo Kogyo, Ford and Nissan for the manufacture of automatic gearboxes. The rotary engine passed Federal tests that year, and exports to the United States began shortly afterwards. The first cars – with both rotary and more conventional powerplants appearing in the line-up – arrived there in the spring of 1970. Within a year, Mazda dealerships were selling vehicles before there was even time to unload them from the transporters.

Following the death of Tsuneji Matsuda in November 1970 (he was 74), the reins were passed to his son, Kohei, the third generation of the Matsuda family to head the company. There was a whole string of important introductions during the early 1970s: the Mazda Capella (RX-2) was followed by the Savanna (RX-3) and, in 1972, the Luce (RX-4) made its debut. Mazda cars were now beginning to outsell trucks year after year. By the end of 1972, cumulative production had reached a staggering five million units, and the Mazda Technical Centre had been established in Irvine, California.

The oil crisis held up a number of interesting projects, such as the X020G 2+2 coupé. Rotary units,

The original Mazda RX-7 – a car that was immensely popular in the US, despite the fuel crisis and unfavourable exchange rates. The car had an excellent competition record in America, too.

some rated up to 200bhp, were being prepared, but the timing, sadly, was all wrong, and sales of rotary-engined models as a whole began to suffer as fuel economy became an overriding consideration for new car buyers. As a result, Toyo Kogyo soon ran into financial troubles and had to turn to the Sumitomo Bank for help to keep the business afloat. The company eventually received the bank's backing, but the Matsuda family lost some of its power in the process.

The RX-7 Savanna
1977 saw the introduction of the Familia (the original GLC/323, powered by a conventional four-stroke engine), which doubtless helped combat the downturn in Mazda sales. However, it was the car launched the following year that was significant to enthusiasts of sporting machinery.

Things were starting to happen in Japan as far as the sports car world was concerned. Nissan had been building the highly-successful Fairlady Z since late 1969, but, during 1978, it took a distinct move upmarket. Mazda had launched the RX-7 (known in Japan as the Savanna) in March 1978, and, in effect, this took the market position of the old Fairlady Z as a cheap but competent sports car, selling for 1,230,000 yen.

As Kohei Matsuda said in late-1977: "A two-seater sports car may well represent the ultimate design compliment for the rotary engine." He was absolutely right. The Mazda marque had already acquired a reputation among motorsport enthusiasts for its sporting

machines, but the rotary-engined RX-7 established the Japanese carmaker all over the world, and signalled a turnaround in the fortunes of the Wankel power unit.

Of course, the RX-7 was admired on the home market as well, and duly received the 'Japanese Car of the Year' award. However, by the time it was officially put on sale, Yoshiki Yamasaki had become the head of the company – the first non-Matsuda family member to do so since 1922.

Revival, and links with Ford
Sales started to pick up again after the introduction of the conventionally powered Familia family car and the immensely popular RX-7. Cumulative production reached ten million vehicles in 1979, but, in November that year, Ford acquired a 24.5 per cent equity stake in Mazda. Within three years, Mazda was marketing Ford brand vehicles through its Autorama sales channel in Japan. This arrangement actually worked both ways, as a number of Mazdas (such as the B-series pick-up) had been badged as Fords in the States, and vehicles were later developed jointly on both sides of the Pacific.

In the meantime, 1980 brought with it the introduction of the front-wheel drive Mazda Familia (also known as the GLC or 323 depending on the market). The Familia was presented with the coveted 1980-1981 'Japanese Car of the Year' award, and over one million had been produced by 1982.

As a matter of interest, Japanese manufacturers built seven million vehicles between them during 1980,

The NA-series MX-5

When the Mazda MX-5 (aka the Roadster or Miata) made its debut at the 1989 Chicago Show, it's fair to say that most marketing folks had written off the lightweight sports car, citing the fact that hardly any were available, and sales of such vehicles were meagre to say the least. But that very point, poor sales of what were basically ageing machines, also had a flipside – a niche market for those brave enough to throw down the gauntlet and develop something more modern for people that put driving enjoyment ahead of practicality or performance figures, which were largely academic in any case.

Mazda was incredibly lucky in that it had a team of enthusiasts who toiled away until each minute detail was exactly in line with the vision of Toshihiko Hirai, the original Chief Engineer who preached the need for the car to promote a feeling akin to the "oneness between horse and rider."

The original car (the NA1) was sold with a B6-series 1.6-litre twin-cam four that delivered 120bhp. The lack of power on paper did not concern Hirai, for he wanted a machine that would deliver enjoyment through control rather than blistering standing-quarter times. Combined with a short-throw five-speed gearbox, an accurate double-wishbone suspension and discs all-round, the package added up to a breath of fresh air – a throwback to simpler times, and

something appreciated by enthusiasts of all ages. To say the new car was a hit is an understatement of epic proportions – the risk had certainly paid off, and the little Mazda duly sparked off a full-blooded revival of the LWS.

In time, options like air conditioning, a hardtop and a limited-slip differential were joined by an automatic transmission, while the V Special (introduced in July 1990) brought with it BRG paint, a tan interior and hood (all-black was the norm), and a selection of wooden trim parts. By this time, of course, the Mazda was already selling in huge numbers in America and Europe.

The first of many limited editions was released in the summer of 1991, followed by specialist M2 models, designed and built by a special team based in Tokyo. July 1993 was a date to remember, though, as that is when the face-lifted NA2 cars made their debut. These were powered by a stronger 1.8-litre BP-type engine delivering 130bhp, but the basic formula was retained – indeed, had it not been for the need to comply with new regulations that added weight to the 1994 MY vehicles, one can safely assume nothing would have changed.

While the M2 project fell by the wayside in 1995, the standard cars were still flying out of showrooms at a healthy rate, the pace helped along by a seemingly endless flow of limited edition models, both at home and abroad. By the time the new generation Roadster (the NB1) had made its debut, at the 1997 Tokyo Show, no less than 431,506 examples of the much-loved NA-series cars had been sold.

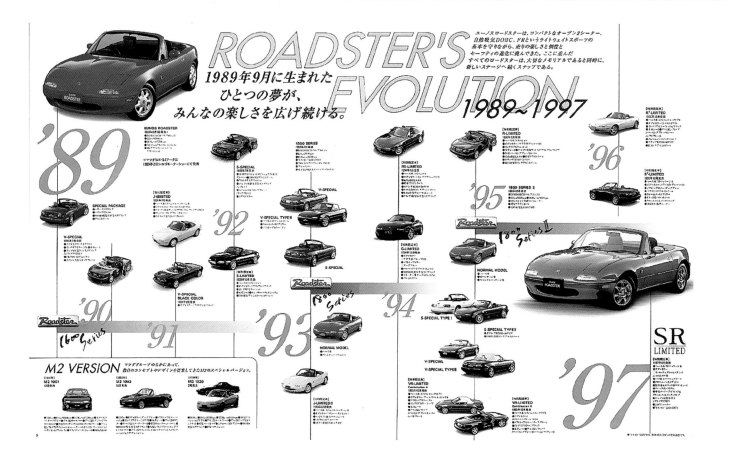

Left: The Eunos trademark associated with the domestic NA-series cars.

Above: The first generation Roadster, also known as the Miata or MX-5. This car single-handedly revived the lightweight sports car (LWS) market after its 1989 debut. Left: Family tree of the first generation (NA-series) MX-5.

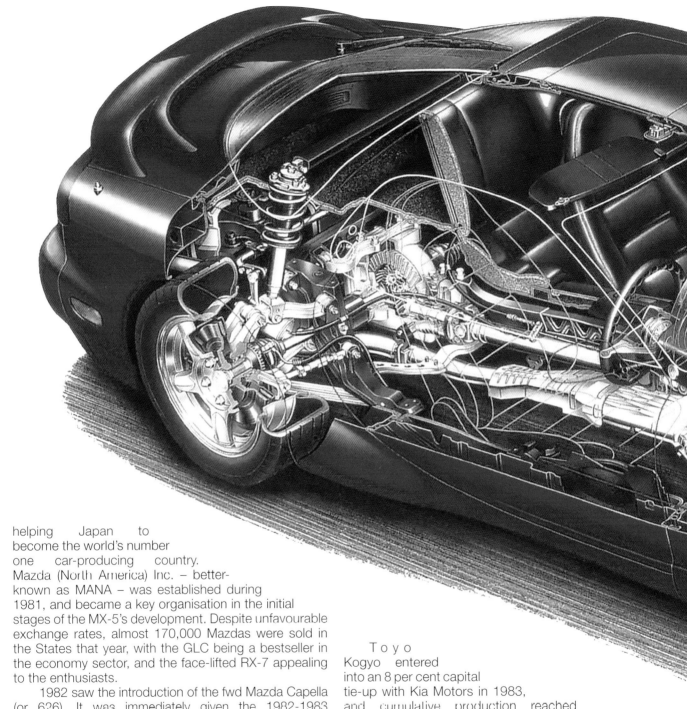

helping Japan to
become the world's number
one car-producing country.
Mazda (North America) Inc. – better-
known as MANA – was established during
1981, and became a key organisation in the initial
stages of the MX-5's development. Despite unfavourable
exchange rates, almost 170,000 Mazdas were sold in
the States that year, with the GLC being a bestseller in
the economy sector, and the face-lifted RX-7 appealing
to the enthusiasts.

1982 saw the introduction of the fwd Mazda Capella
(or 626). It was immediately given the 1982-1983
'Japanese Car of the Year' award in its native country, but
it also received a large number of prestigious accolades
overseas, including being named *Motor Trend* magazine's
1983 'Import Car of the Year.' Sales in America continued
to climb as the Mazda range attracted an ever wider
audience.

Toyo
Kogyo entered
into an 8 per cent capital
tie-up with Kia Motors in 1983,
and cumulative production reached
15 million units. From a very small beginning, the
Mazda marque had grown at great speed, and now had
a range of vehicles that could compete in all markets,
challenging established manufacturers throughout the
world. However, Toyo Kogyo was not yet satisfied with
its achievements ...

Cutaway drawing of the third generation RX-7, launched at the end of 1991, the year in which the Hiroshima concern won the coveted Le Mans 24-hour Race. The last of these fabulous machines was built in August 2002.

Announced in 1991, the life of the elegant MX-6 coupé was coming to an end alongside the NA-series Roadster. On the road car front, they were joined in 1997 by the Mazda Carol, the AZ-Wagon, the Demio (121), the Familia (323), the MS-6/Chronos (626), the Eunos 800 (Xedos 9 or Millenia), the Sentia (929), the MX-3 (Eunos Presso or AZ-3), the RX-7, and MPV.

The Mazda Motor Corporation

The Toyo Kogyo business was renamed the Mazda Motor Corporation on 1 May 1984, with Kenichi Yamamoto elected President shortly after his 62nd birthday. Born in September 1922, the former MD had served Toyo Kogyo for many years, helping the turn the RE engine dream into reality, and had been the company's Chief Engineer since January 1978.

As it happens, Yamamoto was instrumental in allowing the MX-5 project to go ahead, as the second generation RX-7 was about to go upmarket, and a cheaper sports car seemed to make a lot of sense as far as he was concerned, even if the approval of such a beast wasn't met with the same level of enthusiasm in other areas of the boardroom.

The Mazda Technical Research Centre opened in Hiroshima in 1985, building on the work of the oddly-named OGG team. Meanwhile, in the background, development work continued on the new MX-5 convertible, even though its future was far from assured at this stage. Approval had already been given to a new MPV, and the desire to build a new Kei-car meant that funds were tight to say the least. Fortunately, a joint-project with Suzuki on the latter freed up enough of a budget to get the two-seater to market, and the rest, as they say, is history.

Although the recession that followed the boom of the late-1980s naturally hurt the Japanese car manufacturers, it was a change in the local taxation laws and unfavourable exchange rates that did the real damage, especially the latter in Mazda's case. A luxury car division (called Amati) was planned to compete with the Lexus, Infiniti and Acura organizations but, in view of the economic situation, the idea was binned. Yoshihiro Wada, Mazda's President since December 1991, didn't seem overly worried in public, although it came as no surprise to industry followers that Ford's involvement with the company became ever stronger.

One has to feel sorry for Mazda – the oil crisis hurting the RE in the 1970s, then a financial crisis overshadowing an historic win at Le Mans and a new sports car in the shape of the third generation RX-7 that could hold its own against the world's best in the 1990s. On both occasions, potential was blunted by a situation beyond its control.

Ultimately, on 12 April 1996, Ford increased its share in the Japanese company to just over a third, and by the end of 1997, eight of the top 35 positions within Mazda were held by foreigners. At least there was some good news – development work continued on the rotary engine, and there was a new MX-5 waiting in the wings …

Chapter 2

*T*HE SECOND GENERATION

Mazda had obviously found a winning formula with the MX-5 series – sales well in excess of 400,000 units in such a short space of time is testimony to that fact – but it was inevitable that, sooner or later, the popular sports car was going to need a face-lift.

Although sales were still strong in parts of Europe (the UK especially), they were gently falling in America, and quite rapidly in Japan. The first generation (or M1) model could have carried on at these levels, but it was obvious that the older car wouldn't pass the stricter crash regulations planned for 1999.

Mazda, therefore, called upon its Technical Research Centres in Japan (both in Hiroshima and at the Yokohama branch, completed in mid-1987), America (the MRA team in California), and Germany (the European R&D centre, known by the initials MRE, which was completed in May 1990, situated in Oberusel on the outskirts of Frankfurt), to put forward their ideas. The brief was to update the car, enabling it to meet forthcoming regulations, but keeping its character intact.

Speaking in 1990, John Ebenezer (Mazda UK's Chairman at the time) said: "Few people are aware of Mazda's total commitment to producing more than just pedestrian cars, and the Technical Research Centres are essential weapons in achieving this ambition. What makes them so unique and particularly exciting is that the Japanese have insisted upon a high level of local ideas and input. The result is that while most of the personnel in the Hiroshima and Yokohama centres are obviously Japanese, the Irvine and Frankfurt centres are more than 80 per cent staffed by Americans and Europeans, respectively. What is particularly pleasing for me as a Briton is the fact that four of the department heads in Frankfurt are British, who have all, incidentally, been recruited from Porsche ..."

Mazda is quite unusual for a Japanese company in that, of the top 35 positions at the end of 1997, eight were held by foreigners, due mainly to Ford's involvement. One of them, Henry Wallace, joined the Mazda board in 1993, along with two other Ford executives, and became President three years later. He was thus the first *gaijin* (or foreigner) to hold the presidency of a Japanese car company.

It is interesting to note that Ford (which had increased its share in the Japanese company to 33.4 per cent on 12 April 1996, thereby achieving a controlling interest), left alone the Mazda team during the car's development, asking only that the project be "speeded along." It's also interesting that, although sports car sales were in a downward spiral compared to those of RVs and MPVs, Ford still backed the M2

Again, Mazda drew on the talent spread throughout its various design studios around the world in a bid to find the desired shape for the second generation MX-5 (J07E). The Frankfurt office submitted some stunning sketches, although they weren't developed further.

Roadster project, despite 1997 being a bad year financially (share values dropped almost 8 per cent). It was actually a far braver decision to support the M2 than the first generation ever was – there were far more competitors vying for the business of less customers. However, compared to the situation in Korea at that time, the Japanese company had little to worry about ...

A fresh face

Unlike the competition held as part of the OGG project (which ultimately led to the first generation MX-5), there were to be no winners or losers with the second generation; Mazda simply wanted ideas from its various design centres. The whole project was overseen by Martin Leach. Each design centre was given the same brief: keep the car's character intact.

Tom Matano gave an interesting example of how the new car should be designed: "Looking from 100 metres away, a person should recognise the vehicle is a Miata. From 50 metres, it will still appear to be a Miata, but as it gets closer still, they will realize it is the new model."

The amazing thing is that all of the designs were very similar, although, as everyone started from the same point, it's perhaps not so surprising. From sketches, each centre (except the Frankfurt studio) produced full-sized clays which were presented for inspection at a meeting in Hiroshima. The proposal from the Yokohama office fell by the wayside quite quickly, leaving just the Irvine and Hiroshima offerings to choose from. After much deliberation, the MRA design (credited to Ken Saward – an ex-Chrysler man) was the one chosen for further development.

*Above: This series of drawings came from the
Hiroshima studio. Covered headlights were
investigated, but the consensus of opinion was
to go with the exposed lights. Incidentally, the back
looked like a Jaguar XK8 on the pink-coloured sketch,
which was later used as the basis for Hiroshima's full-size clay.*

A front and rear view of Irvine's design. With shades of the original remaining, Irvine's design was nonetheless far more muscular; already strong second generation (M2) features were showing through.

Two views of the clay made to represent the Yokohama design. The author feels that this was an exceptionally pretty car, which, sadly, was rejected.

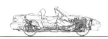

Evolution, not revolution

Tentative development work on the 'full model change' had started in spring 1994, but it wasn't until November 1995 that the project began in earnest, by which time the first batch of mechanical mules was already undergoing extensive testing.

Takao Kijima had been appointed Chief Engineer of the MX-5 in July 1995, meaning that responsibility for the second generation fell on his shoulders. Kijima, who had been with Mazda since 1967, was an important member of the team which developed the first MX-5, and was also highly respected for his work through the years on the RX-7. Incidentally, his predecessor, Shiro Yoshioka, became Chief Chassis Engineer in the Development Centre. Koichi Hayashi, who had worked on the first generation body alongside Matano, was given the job of Chief Designer. Kijima found that the 1.8-litre engine hooked up to an F1-style steering wheel shift was on the cards for the next generation, but he quickly dismissed the idea as unsuitable for a car like the Miata. A new line of development was instigated ...

In May 1997, the excellent Japanese magazine, *Car Graphic*, published an interview with Takao Kijima. A lot of clues were given about what to expect from the new MX-5; for instance, it would definitely continue to have a front engine, rear-wheel drive (FR) layout, and the wheelbase and suspension set-up would stay much the same. The standard use of dual airbags, and the need to meet stricter safety and emissions regulations, was obviously going to increase the car's weight. In fact, at one point it was thought that up

One of the design sketches submitted by the Yokohama office. The front three-quarter view of the same proposal showed that the Yokohama staff wanted to keep the pop-up headlight arrangement.

The first clay produced to represent Hiroshima's proposal. The headlights, it has to be said, looked a little strange on this model, but the front spoiler detailing was very dramatic. The rear lights were quite big, but there were some very delicate lines in the styling; the top of the rear wing was particularly attractive. Note the door lines, which were very similar to those of the first generation model.

The modellers hard at work in California transforming a two-dimensional drawing into a three-dimensional clay.

Right & opposite: The second full-size clay from the Hiroshima team, developed from a one-fifth scale model, and given the 'Theme A' moniker. The air intake and front spoiler were integrated now, and the door lines were made to look more interesting. In addition, the rear combination lights became more elegant, and this, combined with a different bumper shape, made the tail-end appear more substantial.

Right & opposite: The finished second clay from the California team. The headlights were made fractionally longer to incorporate the front indicators, which, in turn, led to adoption of separate side repeaters. The sill, or rocker panel, was given a beefier look, and the bootlid developed a lip spoiler.

Right & opposite: Hiroshima's Theme A model was later refined, with a new air intake and lights, a slightly revised front wing line, a modified trailing edge to the door, and new tail graphics. It was eventually produced in glassfibre (the red car in this batch of pictures), and presented to the Mazda board for evaluation in August 1995.

Right & opposite: The finished clay built using the Ken Saward drawings as the basis. When the three full-sized models, from MRA (Irvine), MRY (Yokohama) and MC (Hiroshima) were reviewed at the start of 1995, this one, and the one from Hiroshima, were chosen for further development.

Right: Work-in-progress at the Irvine facility, leading to the production of the final clay model seen here in the three photographs opposite.

Above: The glassfibre Hiroshima proposal.

The MRA glassfibre model that was selected for further development to ultimately become the second generation MX-5. It is seen here in Hiroshima awaiting the attentions of Hayashi and his team. Note the appearance of flush door handles.

Awesome performance - just as it should be

Gaze upon the fabulous body of the new Mazda MX-5 and it's obvious that here is a car that was born to perform. Turn on the ignition and the resonant sound that greets you then confirms its performance potential in true roadster fashion.

How this performance manifests itself depends on which of the two new engines is selected: either the fast yet frugal 1.6 litre, 110 bhp unit or the higher power 1.8 litre, 140 bhp powerplant. With four valves per cylinder and fuel injection, both deliver masses of low-down torque for instant pick-up from low revs and produce just the sort of spirited response that's expected of a thoroughbred sports car. And, of course, standard in every engine is Mazda's legendary reliability.

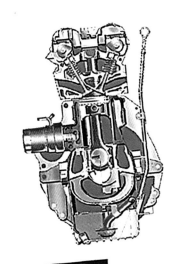

The engine specifications, as seen in the UK catalogue.

The new engines deliver superb performance and exceptional economy.

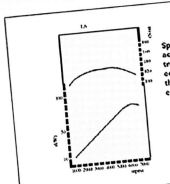

Spirited acceleration, yet tremendously economical: the 110bhp 1.6l engine.

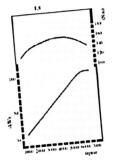

Free-revving, flexible and producing prodigious power: the 140bhp 1.8l engine.

27

A cutaway drawing showing the layout of the second generation model. Incidentally, the 48-litre (10.6 Imperial or 12.7 US gallons) fuel tank capacity was carried over from the NA2 models.

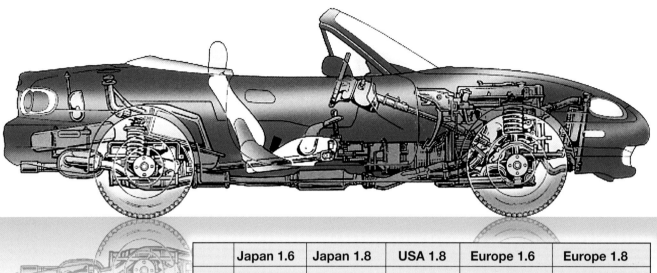

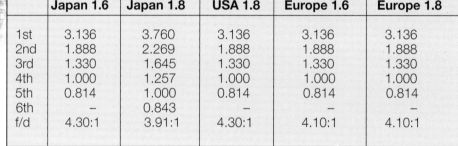

	Japan 1.6	Japan 1.8	USA 1.8	Europe 1.6	Europe 1.8
1st	3.136	3.760	3.136	3.136	3.136
2nd	1.888	2.269	1.888	1.888	1.888
3rd	1.330	1.645	1.330	1.330	1.330
4th	1.000	1.257	1.000	1.000	1.000
5th	0.814	1.000	0.814	0.814	0.814
6th	–	0.843	–	–	–
f/d	4.30:1	3.91:1	4.30:1	4.10:1	4.10:1

Different gear ratios and final-drive specifications.

A word from Koichi Hayashi (Chief Designer on the M2 body) –

Miho Long: "What would you describe as the hardest part of the design?"

Mr Hayashi: "Actually, the toughest part was the very first step – deciding on which direction the design should take.

"We had to make a decision on how to improve a car that was already accepted worldwide, and therefore had to bear in mind how the design of the second generation would fit into the Roadster's history. We also had to consider what sort of design theme was the most suitable expression for a contemporary Mazda sports car.

"I struggled to come to a conclusion regarding how to improve the car, so as a result I decided not to change the image of the first generation too much, keeping the original concept, but at the same time giving the vehicle a more sporty and modern feel."

Miho Long: "Could you tell us what is your favourite part of the body, and why?"

Mr Hayashi: "Definitely the rear fender [wing]. I wanted to give it a dynamic feel, an accent for the whole body. This part of the body surface has a real feeling of tension, yet still has a comfortable atmosphere from any angle – it was finished exactly the way I wanted it. Personally, I love the view one gets of this area from the rear view mirror when I'm driving!"

Takao Kijima – Chief Engineer for the second generation MX-5. During the vehicle's development, he tested the Fiat Barchetta, MGF and the new Alfa Spider, but stated that he failed to feel the desired "oneness between car and driver" that he wanted.

to 60kg (132lb) would be added. However, a light package was crucial; according to Kijima it was "hard work to find the balance between strength and weight, but to make an all-aluminium chassis like the [Lotus] Elise would make the car too expensive."

Kijima also wrote an essay outlining the aims of the design team. It read as follows: "In the eight years since the Rebirth of the Lightweight Sports Roadster in the form of the Mazda MX-5, more than 430,000 agile and friendly roadsters have been delivered to the world's enthusiasts, rekindling a powerful flame among them for exhilarating open-air motoring and imparting the joy of 'Oneness between the Car and Driver.'

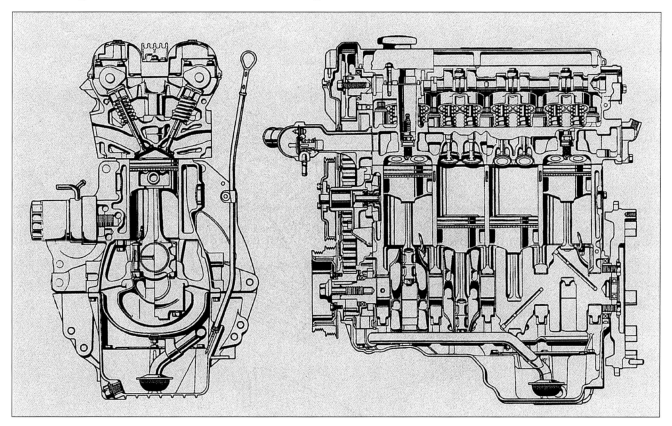

Cutaway drawings of the 1.8-litre BP-ZE (RS) power unit.

"We at Mazda are firm believers in continuous improvement. A sports car must be thoroughly contemporary and up to date, incorporating the latest technological developments. To rest on your laurels is to stagnate and fall behind. The original MX-5 has thus been constantly refined, including two major updates and numerous improvements, to answer our customers' expectations and requirements.

"The last decade of the century has seen giant leaps in technology, particularly in electronics, but also in the design, development and manufacture of the automobile. At the same time, society's concern about safety and environmental issues has become more acute. We decided that the MX-5 must progress to meet the challenges of the 21st century. We will accomplish this by further enhancing the lightweight open sports car's dynamics and meeting all social requirements.

"There was one fundamental principle guiding Mazda's design and engineering team for the new MX-5's personality: 'We must value and assert the MX-5's inborn Soul, and train, strengthen and refine the Body.' The new car required no conceptual revision. Enhance the virtue of the compact, lightweight, two-seat open sports car, and offer a sports car unparalleled in ownership delight and driving pleasure, to people of all walks of life, young and young at heart. We pursued new dimensions in open-air motoring, fun-to-drive and styling.

"With the objectives clearly established, we pursued three key areas of development:

1) Joy of open-air motoring, in comfort and ease: The new MX-5 is to be enjoyed primarily as an open sports car at all speeds and even in winter, barring extremely inclement weather. We were able to accomplish this goal with innovative design and features.

2) True sports car driving fun: 'Oneness of the Car and Driver' enables the driver to fully exploit the new MX-5's exciting, natural and safe performance potential. The development team's aim of instinctive 'drive-by-wish' precision was realized. Sounds are important ingredients in sports car driving. Thus, the new MX-5's engine and exhaust are tuned to delight the ears of the driver, passenger and onlookers.

3) Thoroughly modern yet unmistakable MX-5 styling: The instantly recognisable exterior design carries the lineage of the original MX-5 in a balanced, masculine manner, and the interior stimulates enthusiasm the instant you climb behind the wheel.

"The car's everyday practicality has also been improved, including a larger and more usable luggage compartment. Safety has been greatly enhanced by incorporating a highly rigid body structure and a standard dual SRS airbag system for all models.

The final prototype, photographed in the Hiroshima studio. The basic styling was obviously settled on very early in the proceedings, as only detail changes were made on each of the full-size models that followed on from Ken Saward's original drawings.

"With this new model, we believe that we have extended the enjoyment of the fun of the lightweight sports car to a much larger audience.

"We fully utilized the latest Mazda Digital Innovation system (MDI), to incorporate numerous technological advancements into the design, to aid development, and to further improve build quality. The creation of an automobile is ultimately the work of people. And our team dedicated all its effort to ensuring that the sporting Soul of the original MX-5 now dwells within the safe and strong new Body."

Kijima felt it was important to further improve the car's best points and not allow the areas in which it was weak to lose ground against the competition. He had actually consulted Hirai on a number of aspects concerning the project, and also tested all the vehicles from competitors that had come onto the market since the introduction of the Eunos Roadster, noting their strengths and shortcomings. In essence, he wanted to enhance the Mazda's performance, handling, sound and driving sensations, whilst keeping the car affordable.

Engine

Kijima's interview in *Car Graphic* promised a 1.8-litre engine with a lightened flywheel (the 1.8-litre gave a better match for cars with automatic transmission),

while a 1.6-litre unit would be available in Europe, giving the benefit of lower insurance premiums. The exhaust note had again been tuned (noise limits caused a few problems here), and there was also a hint of a six-speed manual gearbox.

With a number of revisions, it was hoped that the existing 1839cc BP-ZE (RS) unit would produce 145bhp at 6500rpm, while the 1597cc B6-ZE (RS) engine was given a target of 125bhp at the same revs. This latter figure represented about 10 per cent more power than before, if the original 1.6-litre specification is taken as the starting point.

After the intake and exhaust system was refined (the Variable Intake Control System – or VICS – was employed) under the direction of Yoshiaki Dairaku, and different pistons (to give a higher compression ratio), camshaft profiles and a remapped ECU were adopted, the Japanese catalogue confirmed that these targets had been met.

European specifications, however, suggested a shortfall of 5bhp on the 1.8, and no less than 15bhp on the smaller engine. In the American market, the 1.8-litre four-cylinder unit's maximum power output was quoted at 140bhp at 6500rpm, with 119lbft of torque at 5500rpm.

Once again, the exhaust note was tuned to give the new model a sporting bark, although, because

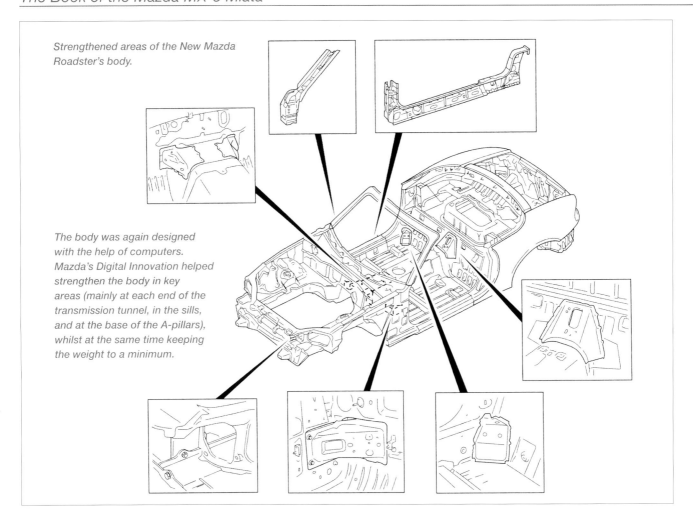

Strengthened areas of the New Mazda Roadster's body.

The body was again designed with the help of computers. Mazda's Digital Innovation helped strengthen the body in key areas (mainly at each end of the transmission tunnel, in the sills, and at the base of the A-pillars), whilst at the same time keeping the weight to a minimum.

of noise regulations, European versions were made substantially quieter than their Japanese and American counterparts.

Drivetrain

Kijima's hint at a six-speed gearbox became reality but, sadly, only for the 1.8-litre cars for the home market. (There was talk of the possibility of a six-speed for the year 2000 in the US, perhaps even with an uprated engine, but it was not a foregone conclusion.) As the press release noted: "The type BP 1.8-litre engine is equipped with a new six-speed manual transmission. The sixth gear performs as an overdrive, contributing to sportier driving with optimum performance including revving and acceleration at higher speeds.

"Both six-speed and five-speed manual transmissions use the short-stroke type stick-shift and promise quick shifting with a flick of the wrist. The transmission achieves higher rigidity from the improved internal synchronized system, producing quick, yet precise, handling even during severe shifting."

The six speed gearbox (designated type Y16M-D, and jointly developed with the Aisin concern) brought the gears closer, of course, which would silence the critics who thought the difference in revs from second to third – and third to fourth, in particular – was too great on the original car, considering how high up the rev range peak torque came in. The six-speed unit came with a single dry plate 215mm (8.5in) diameter hydraulically operated clutch.

The five-speed manual gearbox was of the M15M-D type, incidentally, and was linked to a 200mm (7.9in) clutch. While a single piece propshaft was used to take power to the back axle in all cases, gear ratios and final-drive specifications were different for the various markets.

Naturally, the electronically controlled, four-speed automatic gearbox (type SB4A-EL) had different ratios

again, but it should be noted that, in Japan, the 1.6-litre cars had a 4.30:1 final-drive, while the 1.8s had a 4.10:1 unit. The 4.10:1 ratio was also used in America, but the automatic option was not listed for Europe. A semi-automatic transmission was apparently not even considered; although quite fashionable, it was deemed not pure enough for a back-to-basics sports car.

A Torsen limited-slip differential came on the manual 1.6-litre Special Package and manual 1.8-litre cars in Japan, and as part of the Popular Equipment

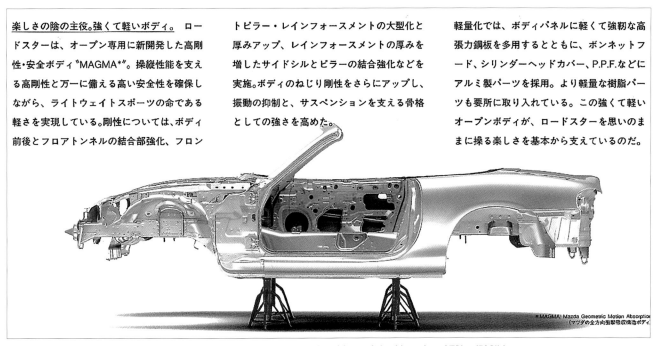

楽しさの陰の主役。強くて軽いボディ。　ロードスターは、オープン専用に新開発した高剛性・安全ボディ"MAGMA*"。操縦性能を支える高剛性と万一に備える高い安全性を確保しながら、ライトウェイトスポーツの命である軽さを実現している。剛性については、ボディ前後とフロアトンネルの結合部強化、フロントピラー・レインフォースメントの大型化と厚みアップ、レインフォースメントの厚みを増したサイドシルとピラーの結合強化などを実施。ボディのねじり剛性をさらにアップし、振動の抑制と、サスペンションを支える骨格としての強さを高めた。軽量化では、ボディパネルに軽くて強靭な高張力鋼板を多用するとともに、ボンネットフード、シリンダーヘッドカバー、P.P.F.などにアルミ製パーツを採用。より軽量な樹脂パーツも要所に取り入れている。この強くて軽いオープンボディが、ロードスターを思いのままに操る楽しさを基本から支えているのだ。

*MAGMA: Mazda Geometric Motion Absorption
（マツダの全方向衝撃吸収構造ボディ）

A finished monocoque. The new body-in-white weighed in at just 272kg (598lb).

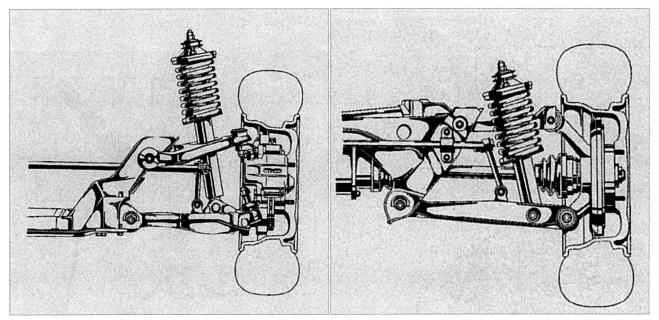

The front suspension.

The rear suspension.

The first S1 prototype to be completed, January 1997. Road testing began almost straight away, with the S1s taking the place of the earlier 'Mechanical Prototypes' or engineering mules.

Package in the States. In Europe, it came on the higher grade 1.8-litre machines as standard. The PPF transmission and drivetrain brace was carried over from the first generation.

Chassis

Koji Tsuji was put in charge of the chassis, and to quote from the Tokyo Show press release: "The front engine, rear-drive layout is maintained, achieving an ideal front and rear weight distribution and optimum enjoyment of control. The engine is mounted midship behind the front axle. The battery and [spare] tyre are placed under the trunk floor. This provides a lower centre of gravity and increased trunk space. Decreasing the front overhang weight and placing all the heaviness as close to the vehicle centre as possible, allowed us to achieve superb yaw inertia moment and ideal 50:50 weight distribution.

"The new Roadster adopts a further refined double-wishbone suspension, which was well-known on the first generation. The carefully tuned suspension geometry was completely reviewed to optimize driving pleasure ... while adding to the vehicle's driving stability. The new damper and coil spring units are individually off-set mounted to minimize transmission of road noise to the body.

"The four-wheel disc brake system is ventilated in front and solid at the rear. The brake system provides precise braking performance.

"The vehicle has rack-and-pinion steering. With the lock-to-lock 2.6 turns, it creates a direct yet quick handling feel. The overlapping effects of the re-adjusted suspension settings and reduced yaw inertia moment achieve extraordinary manoeuverability."

One or two points need further explanation. The new suspension settings made the car understeer less, making it much easier to drift through corners. Standard anti-roll bar diameters were 22mm (0.87in) at the front, 11mm (0.43in) at the rear. However, Japanese spec 1.6-litre models had a 19mm (0.75in) bar up front, while the US Sports Package and home market RS grade had 12mm (0.47in) bars at the back to compliment the stiffer set-up adopted on those vehicles.

As for the brakes, diameters (at 255mm, or 10.0in,

S1 prototypes being built up by hand in the Hiroshima workshops.

up front and 251mm, or 9.9in, at the back) were the same as those found on the last of the first generation cars, while four-sensor, three-channel ABS was available but rarely standard (see the next chapter).

Power-assisted steering came on most cars (again, the next chapter outlines the various specifications), American models were listed with 3.2 turns lock-to-lock on the standard rack, or 2.7 with the speed sensitive power steering.

The wheels were revised yet again, with pressed steel or light alloy options available. The five-spoke alloy wheels came in either 14- or 15-inch guise, but both designs looked very similar. The details of those supplied to the various markets are covered in the following chapter.

Body

Hayashi was basically given a free hand, but he said: "Before full-fledged development began, we tried out different approaches with a view to changing the image during designer training programmes, and on several other occasions. But we decided that the lightweight sports spirit of the original model should not and could not be changed. After much debate, we reached the conclusion that we should simply polish up the spirit of the first generation to create the next generation roadster. Ultimately, all of the proposals submitted by our design centres carried over the image of the original model with a more dynamic style."

He added: "I wanted to let the feeling of the old model live on, because I thought it didn't need changing to any great extent. The original, in the mould of a 1960s British lightweight sports car, was perfect. However, the new body is more three-dimensional and muscular, with some exciting elements. The rich shapes can be viewed from any angle."

The new body incorporated the Mazda Advanced Impact Distrbution and Absorption System, which helped increase passenger safety in the event of an accident. The front and rear crumple zones effectively absorbed impact energy from both directions. Beefier sills (or rockers) minimized body distortion in the case of a side impact, aided by twin bars inside the door panels.

At the same time, this enhanced body rigidity provided an excellent basis for the suspension; reinforcement of the suspension's mounting points naturally had a direct effect on handling. After almost 30,000 stress measurements were taken on the all-steel unitary body, it was estimated that overall rigidity had increased by some 38 per cent.

In all, only around 40 per cent of the new body was carried over from the M1 roadster. Virtually all of the panels were new, including the floorpan, but, due to the limited budget, the original windscreen, windscreen surround, and most of the cowl were retained – this at least meant that the first generation model's hard-top could still be used with the second generation car.

The wings were given a more muscular shape (adding a little to the overall width of the vehicle, even though it went against Kijima's express wish "not to add a single millimetre") with the lines flowing over into the bonnet, while the doors now had a large radius curve at the bottom of the trailing edge (a feature found on the RX-7), and Shunji Tanaka's original door handles were dropped in favour of more modern items finished in body colour.

The sill panels looked heavier than before (as Tom Matano put it, they have "more drama"), merging with the leading edge of the door to give a distinctive styling feature. The crease was deleted between the wheels, but there were still remnants of the M1's centre line where the bumpers joined the body.

The familiar pop-up headlights were deleted in favour of fixed ellipsoid lenses in a bid to save weight at the front. Losing the pop-up lights shed 5.6kg (12lb). This was not only the biggest single saving gained from the weight-cutting operation, it also improved the car's aerodynamics (there was quite a dramatic difference in Cd readings once the old lights were brought up into the raised position, but with fixed lights, this was no longer a problem).

Moving back, the centre edge of the bootlid incorporated a duck-tail lip to improve aerodynamics (as well as the high level rear brake light, the new Mazda badge and number plate lights), while up front, an aluminium bonnet was employed once again, despite the need to save money. The air intake was larger than before, and both bumpers looked less dainty – the styling lines found in the sills continued through to the lower edge of the bumpers.

Interestingly, the rear panel that carries the number plate and badging was now part of the bumper assembly instead of a separate piece. (Or more correctly, two separate pieces from a manufacturing

Three of the many design proposals put forward for the M2 interior.

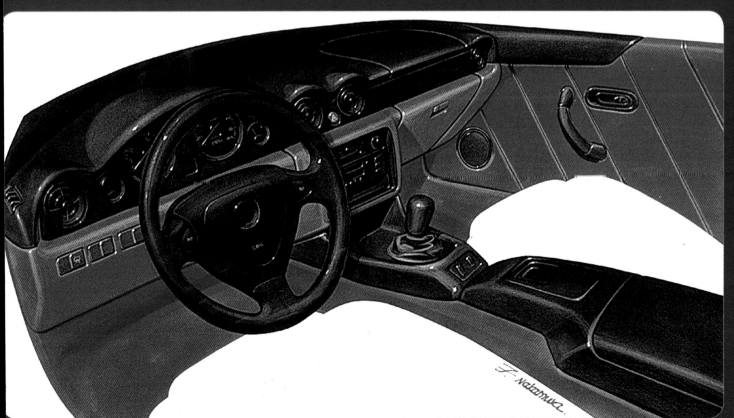

point of view, as the first generation cars for the home market had their own panel which fitted neatly around Japanese registration plates – now all markets had the same specification.)

In addition to the front lights being changed, those at the rear were also modified, but not quite as drastically. The main point of the exercise was to incorporate the rear foglight into the design (for the markets that required one), thus removing the need for a separate item mounted under the bumper.

The manual operation of the hood was kept in order to avoid the weight of electric motors and the complicated mechanism that a power operated hood would require, while the door mirrors were now sharper-looking items – longer and narrower.

Overall dimensions of the new Roadster read as follows: the leading measurements were length 3955mm (155.7in); width 1680mm (66.1in); height 1235mm (48.6in), and wheelbase 2265mm (89.2in). Ground clearance was 135mm (5.3in), while the front and rear track were 1405 and 1430mm (55.3 and 56.3in) respectively, signifying a 10mm (0.4in) increase in the rear track. The body was therefore slightly shorter, but 5mm (0.2in) wider; the height and wheelbase were unchanged. With the hood up, the Cd was recorded at 0.36 (an improvement of 0.02 over the original).

The possibility of a coupé was raised during the *Car Graphic* interview with Kijima, to which the disappointing reply was "I don't think so." It was dismissed on the grounds that it destroyed the aim of making a light open car if there was to be a coupé, too, which employs completely different construction methods. One had to take a dedicated approach. Indeed, Takaharu 'Koby' Kobayakawa had stated from the outset that there would never be a third generation RX-7 cabriolet for much the same reasons.

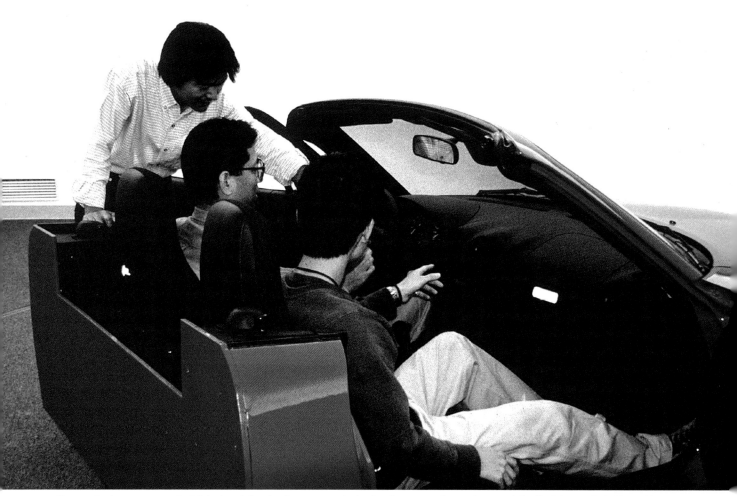

Once a design was accepted, interior styling bucks were made to check ergonomics and general 'feel' of the cockpit. Hayashi-san can be seen at the wheel in this picture.

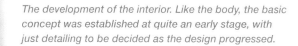

The development of the interior. Like the body, the basic concept was established at quite an early stage, with just detailing to be decided as the design progressed.

The production interior, as seen here on a lhd car for the European mainland.

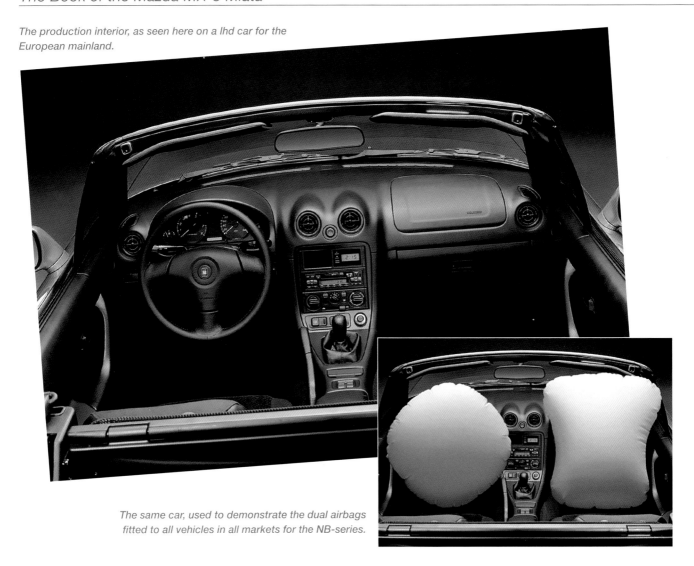

The same car, used to demonstrate the dual airbags fitted to all vehicles in all markets for the NB-series.

This was a shame, nonetheless, as many had admired the M-Coupé; at the time of its debut in 1996, it was said that, if reaction was favourable – which it was – it might go into production. In reality, it is probably fair to say that Mazda didn't want the possibility of an MX-5 coupé stealing sales from the RX-7, especially given the fact that the sports car market was still shrinking in all corners of the globe.

Interior

Work on the interior was done solely in Hiroshima, with the main objective being to cut manufacturing costs, whilst at the same time giving the cockpit a feeling of greater quality. To quote the press release handed out at the Tokyo Show: "With almost identical interior dimensions to the first generation, the new Roadster offers comfortably close interior space, enhancing the feeling of oneness between car and driver.

"The design of the T-shaped instrument panel is inherited from the first generation. The centre console wraps around both driver and passenger thanks to the low seat position. All the individual round gauges are gathered in a simple semi-circle cluster. The six-speed manual transmission model features a unique tachometer and speedmeter with needles pointing at the six o'clock start position. The steering wheel is a jointly-developed Nardi small-diameter three-spoke type with Supplemental Restraint System (SRS) airbag. The high-back bucket-type seats are superior in holding capability.

"Enlarged storage space in the door pockets and the centre console box provide greater overall storage capacity, and dual cup holders in the rear console box add practicality. The Roadster's exclusive audio system, designed in co-operation with Bose, creates a stereo environment even during open driving. The

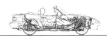

speakers' thin and lightweight construction also contributes to decreased overall vehicle weight without sacrificing performance."

The main difference was the more integrated look of the centre console, with the centre vents becoming part of the main fascia. Although the instrument layout was much the same, the odometer was now a digital readout. The 1.6 and 1.8 had different speedos and tachometers on the home market, with the smaller engined model's needles starting from the traditional eight o'clock position, as did all cars destined for export.

Incidentally, speedometers were calibrated to 180kph in Japan (something found on all recent home market models, from all manufacturers); those for the UK and USA were marked up to 150mph, while cars destined for Continental Europe had 240kph speedos.

Finishing touches

Kijima was of the opinion that although looks were naturally important, it was driving sensations that should be considered the number one priority. Chassis testing was carried out by Masashi Oda on the second batch of mules (completed in mid-1996) and S1 prototypes, with testing as a whole overseen by Takashi Takeshita, Vice-Chief of the Experimental Department.

Vehicle development took place all over the world, mainly on mock-ups using the first generation body. It is interesting to note that Oda was at first against the six-speed gearbox in the prototype stages, but, nonetheless, it was eventually perfected.

Although Mazda insisted on one-handed operation of the soft-top, in reality, the material used in the old rear window meant it needed to be unzipped before the lid was dropped to avoid damaging it. The new model's glass rear screen was a vast improvement, as it was now possible to unclip the catches and let the hood fall backwards without worry. Despite the heavier glass screen, the hood as a whole was actually around 1kg (2lb) lighter than its predecessor.

The added strength of the new body made the cockpit brace bar unnecessary, but there was another interesting feature behind the seats – a windblocker (or anti-draft panel), as found on the RX-7 Cabriolet. Kobayakawa, its inventor, had requested one for the original MX-5, but Hirai insisted that he wanted passengers to "play with the wind." As a die-hard open car man, Koby, like the author, tends to drop the hood whatever the season (after all, what's the point having a soft-top if you use it like a coupé all year round!), and asked if Hirai had ever played with a winter wind! The answer was no, but Hirai would not be moved, and it wasn't until the second generation model that this simple – but effective – device would be fitted

to the little roadster. Mazda's unique "Windblocker is incorporated behind the seats to reduce wind turbulence entering the leg room from behind during open driving. The result, is an improved heater, which enhances comfort during open winter driving."

In its lightest home market form, the new Roadster weighed in at 1000kg (2200lb). This meant a 60kg (132lb) increase compared to the original, but it was only 20kg (44lb) more than the basic 1.8-litre Series II model. Kijima was justifiably proud of this achievement, reiterating that a light package was absolutely crucial.

The pilot build took place in Hiroshima, with these earliest cars once again having the S1 designation; the run was completed in January 1997. Thanks to the use of DPA (Digital Pre-Assembly, which allows the cars to be 'built' on computer before tackling the real thing), very little rectification was needed before the car entered production.

Eager anticipation

By the end of 1996, speculation was rife about the new model. *Complete Car* magazine in the UK noted in September: "Mazda's MX-5 will be in for a face-lift by the end of next year, with the now old-fashioned pop-up lights being dropped. The revamp will be subtle ... but further ahead Mazda may also consider a more muscular, performance version of the car as an image-booster."

As early as July 1997, several British magazines were carrying details of the new MX-5 after somebody put a Mazda promotional video on the Internet. The new headlight arrangement was obvious from the various spy shots that were published after the leak, but, much to Mazda's dismay, virtually everyone knew the full details of the MX-5's replacement months before the planned launch at the 1997 Tokyo Show.

Although specifications were fairly clear by now, no-one outside the company knew what the car was like to drive. It was obvious that Mazda was not going to let the new car fall below the standard set by the first generation model, but it would be reassuring to know for sure.

Writing for *Road & Track* in September 1997, Thos L Bryant teased enthusiasts with the following statement: "In the spring, Mazda Motors of America's Vice-President of Public Affairs, Jay Amestoy, suggested that a small group of us should go to Japan to meet with the people designing and engineering the upcoming new Miata ... I am sworn to secrecy, but I will allow as how the new version is sure to please."

The scene was set ...

Interior of the new model. Note the 'Windblocker' behind the seats, designed to stop drafts. The hard-top anchorage points on the rear deck were carried over from the previous model.

A rear view of the second generation car. Note the new lighting arrangement (this being a Japanese spec vehicle, it is equipped with twin reversing lights – one in each cluster).

Although only 5mm (0.2in) wider in reality, the new car looked far wider and lower visually. As Martin Leach (the MD in charge of Product Planning, Design & Programs), said: "It's got more presence." Clinics had been held in both America and Japan, the car's biggest markets.

Testing at the Miyoshi Proving Ground. As well as being put through their paces in Japan, the S1s were also shipped to America and Europe for extensive testing and evaluation.

While the original 1600 looked very basic in the luggage area, the first 1800 had a well-trimmed boot. The second generation model's luggage compartment was also carpeted, but capacity had increased slightly to 144 litres (5.1 cu ft) – an increase of around 15 per cent. However, with the spare wheel and battery moving below the boot floor, the space provided was far more useful.

American advertising showing the all-new 1999 model year Miata. The American press release stated: "It lifts your spirit and renews your soul." The US press launch was held on Big Island, Hawaii.

Production at Hiroshima. Note the new winged Mazda symbol on the nose (it also appeared on the bootlid), said to represent "Mazda spreading its wings as it soars into the future."

A left-hand drive model fresh from the production line and undergoing a final series of checks.

Chapter 3

THE NEW CAR
TAKES A BOW

Despite various leaks threatening to spoil the build-up, the official launch of the new model at the 32nd Tokyo Show was still a big event for the world's media. The press conference was held on 22 October, three days before the doors at Makuhari Messe opened to the public.

In the highlights booklet handed out at the Tokyo Show, the new Mazda Roadster (the Eunos name had been dropped), was given top billing in the Mazda section: "The all-new Roadster makes its world debut at the Tokyo Motor Show. This superb car embodies the enduring appeal of authentic lightweight sports cars.

"The new Roadster employs a lightweight, compact and highly-rigid two-seater open body. Its exterior features modern sports car styling carried over from the original Roadster model. Under the hood, Mazda offers a choice of either a 1.8-litre or 1.6-litre engine with enhanced power. These engines work in harmony with the car's advanced chassis to improve the driving feel, responsive handling and smooth ride.

"The 1.8-litre-engined model comes with a close-ratio six-speed manual transmission. The new Roadster also features the highly-rigid MAGMA safety body."

Mazda had two of the new Roadsters on display - a gold coloured model (a stunning shade that was used extensively in early publicity shots from around the time of the launch) and one finished in a tasteful dark green.

However, apart from the new MX-5s and a solitary RX-7, the theme of the Mazda stand very much reflected the fashion of the time, with MPVs and estate cars dominating. The management couldn't be blamed for this, however, as it was

The launch of the second generation Mazda Roadster at the 1997 Tokyo Show. This photograph was taken by the author on the first press day. Note the tiny chin spoiler fitted to the 1.8-litre cars.

Mazda actually had two of the new Roadsters on display at the 1997 Tokyo Show – the gold-coloured model on the rotating stand, and this top-of-the-range VS in Grey Green Mica mounted high up in the centre of the display.

the strongest sector of the market in Japan as the millennium loomed, while sports cars were in danger of becoming a dying breed. Perhaps this was another reason Mazda didn't go too crazy with a brand new design; it was more prudent to stick with a proven winner.

The press release issued at the show (but dated 15 October) read as follows: "Defined as a new vehicle to be marketed in the future, the all-new Mazda Roadster will be exhibited. Since its world debut in 1989, the first generation Mazda Roadster has been [widely] touted as the best two-seater lightweight roadster in the world. The new Roadster inherits virtues of the first generation and balances all the strong points of top-down driving fun with superb sports car performance and incomparable styling."

The brochure handed out at the Tokyo Show listed all of the salient points of the new Roadster.

Despite having the MS-X, MV-X and SW-X concept cars at the Tokyo Show, it was the new Roadster that made the cover of Mazda's brochure for the event.

The first Japanese brochure for the second generation Roadster. The ubiquitous gold colour (known by different names around the world) was used extensively in build-up publicity and launch material.

It also listed the following nine points:

1. The dimensions of the new Mazda Roadster are 3955mm [155.7in] in overall length, 1680mm [66.1in] in overall width, 1235mm [48.6in] in overall height and 2265mm [89.2in] in wheelbase. Only the overall width is 5mm [0.2in] greater than its predecessor.

2. The basic layout maintains the front engine, rear-drive layout achieving an ideal front and rear weight distribution. The engine is mounted midship behind the axle [i.e. quite far back in the engine bay].

3. Carrying on the design motif recognizable as the Roadster at a glance, the new Roadster is designed to offer sportier, aggressive and dynamic styling in a three-dimensional form.

4. Either 1.8-litre or 1.6-litre in-line, four-cylinder dohc 16v engines are available. With refinement of the intake and exhaust systems, both engines have improved output and torque, enhanced revving characteristics, and greater acceleration response.

5. The 1.8-litre-engined model features a newly-developed, six-speed manual transmission which optimizes engine speed and acceleration characteristics at high revs.

6. The double-wishbone suspension at the front and rear is further enhanced. Through reviewing the geometry and fine tuning, the driving stability of the new Roadster was refined for more fun driving.

7. By incorporating a glass window with defogger, the view through the rear window was greatly improved. By dropping the zipper around the vinyl rear window, [the hood's] open and close operations were eased, while the overall weight of the soft-top was reduced.

8. The highly rigid and safe body Mazda Advanced Impact Distribution and Absorption System achieves enhanced collision safety (also known as MAGMA or Mazda Geometric Motion Absorption). The well-managed body torsion and vibration as a result of increase in the body rigidity contribute to the superb driving stability of the new Roadster.

9. In addition to the driver's and passenger's SRS (Supplemental Restraint System) airbags, the seatbelts are equipped with an automatic tension function that regulates tension force against a certain level of impact with the occupants.

Of course, Mazda no longer had the convertible market to itself, and more cars were joining the MX-5 and

its new competitors all the time. Announced at the 1997 Tokyo Show alongside the new model from Hiroshima, the Toyota MR-S was an indirect replacement for the MR2, designed to compete head-on with the MX-5; although the 1997 vehicle was a concept model, it would go on to star in many fascinating comparison tests with the Mazda Roadster after it went into production. Another debutante at Makuhari Messe that year was the Suzuki C2 – a lightweight open car powered by a 250bhp, 1.6-litre V8. The future definitely looked interesting ...

The home market

As usual, the Japanese market had an extensive line-up of models. The 1.6-litre range included a basic five-speed model, the M Package and Special Package. Both of these latter versions could be bought with a five-speed manual gearbox or four-speed automatic transmission. ABS brakes came as standard with the automatic Roadsters, and were an option on the manual M Package and Special Package cars. All 1.6s came with Mazda's own four-spoke steering wheel, and the Special Package was equipped with power door mirrors.

As for the 1.8-litre car, this was available in three different specifications – the S, RS and VS. These came with a six-speed manual gearbox, but the four-speed automatic transmission could be specified on the S and VS. An ABS braking system was included in the price on all automatic 1.8-litre cars, and an option on each of the manual models.

All 1.8s came with electrically-adjusted door mirrors and a Nardi three-spoke steering wheel; that on the S and RS was leather-wrapped, while the VS had a wood-rimmed item with matching gearknob and handbrake lever handle. Polished treadplates were standard on the RS and VS, and the latter also came with a CD player straight from the factory. Incidentally, manual 1.8-litre models had a unique set of gauges featuring red pointer needles instead of white ones.

All cars came with air conditioning and a driver's footrest, and all but the basic grade had power-assisted steering, electric windows, the Windblocker device, and an automatic aerial, although only the VS came with a stereo as standard – a Bose radio/CD unit that could be ordered as an extra on the RS and Special Package. It was the same situation with the remote controlled central locking (standard on the VS, optional on the RS and Special Package), and a navigation system could be specified as a cost option on the same three grades.

Five-spoke alloy wheels were standard on the 1.6-litre Special Package and the three 1.8-litre grades, although the sizes were different – 185/60 HR14 tyres mounted on 6J x 14 rims was the norm, but the RS came with lightweight 195/50 VR15 Michelin tyres and 6J x 15 alloys to complement its uprated suspension (including Bilstein dampers and a tower brace bar); the basic 1.6 and M Package had 185/60 tyres on 5.5J x 14 pressed steel wheels. Likewise, a Torsen limited-slip differential came with the same range of vehicles, but only when specified in manual guise.

Overall weights ranged from 1000 to 1060kg (2200 to 2332lb), whilst prices, up a fraction on those of the NA2, started at 1,819,000 yen for the basic 1.6-litre model, rising to 2,665,000 yen for the top VS models. The sporty RS was slightly cheaper than the equivalent VS model, as the VS had a higher level of trim. Sales started in January 1998 through both Mazda and Anfini dealerships – the Eunos sales channel no longer existed.

Standard exterior colours on the 1.6-litre cars included Classic Red, Highlight Silver Metallic and Chaste White. By opting for the Special Package or M Package, three more options became available: Evolution Orange

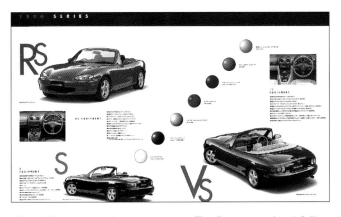

The 1800 series for the home market. The first generation 1.6-litre cars carried the NA6CE chassis designation, whereas 1.8-litre models were identified by the NA8C prefix. For the second generation, the smaller engined car carried the NB6C code, whilst 1.8-litre vehicles were identified by the NB8C chassis number.

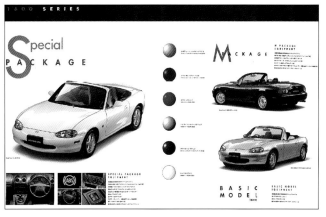

The Japanese 1600 range, as seen in the first catalogue released for the new model. With a 9.4:1 compression ratio, the 1.6-litre engine produced 125bhp at 6500rpm, and 105lbft of torque at 5000rpm.

A series of four advertisements for the new Roadster. Each describes a notable feature, such as the MAGMA body, six-speed transmission, all-round double-wishbone suspension, and the traditional FR layout.

Mica, Twilight Blue Mica, and Brilliant Black. In all cases, the trim was finished in black. Twilight Blue Mica, Brilliant Black and Chaste White could be specified on all 1.8-litre models. The RS and S grades were also available in Evolution Orange Mica (the gold shade that Mazda used in most of its publicity material), Classic Red and Highlight Silver Metallic, while the VS was offered in Grey Green Mica. Again, interior trim was in black, except for the VS which came with tan leather trim and a tan coloured hood.

On the corporate side of things, James E. Miller was announced as Mazda's new President in November 1997, taking the place of Henry Wallace. Miller, the company's former Vice-President, had joined Ford in 1973, although his work had brought him close to the Hiroshima marque for the best part of a decade before his new appointment.

The second generation Stateside

The 1998 Detroit Show (which opened on 10 January) saw the official American launch of the second generation Miata (although it had appeared at Los Angeles a week before), tagged as a 1999 model year car – there would be no 1998 models.

Richard Beattie, President of Mazda North America, said: "The weather outside may be cold and dreary, but with the introduction of our new Miata, things are heating up at Mazda. As good as the original Miata was, this new 1999 Miata is better in every single way. We fully expect it to remain the best-selling two-seat roadster on the planet."

The press release stated: "The car that almost single-handedly revived the two-seat open roadster market around the world arrived in Detroit today as Mazda executives unveiled the all-new 1999 Miata at the 1998 North American International Auto Show. The new Miata, which features a more powerful engine, dramatically restyled body, redesigned interior and improved handling, goes on sale in Mazda dealerships early in 1998.

"The new 1999 Mazda Miata features a more powerful 140bhp 1.8-litre dohc four-cylinder engine, improved four-wheel double-wishbone suspension, more aggressively styled body and a redesigned interior. The body of the new Miata is more rigid for improved handling, yet it weighs the same as its predecessor. The easy-to-use folding top is even easier to operate and now uses a glass rear window with built-in defroster, a feature not found on several convertibles costing much more.

"The new Mazda Miata may not be on sale yet, but the editors of *Car & Driver* magazine are already hailing it as one of the '10 Best Cars' in the publication's January 1998 issue. This is nothing new for the Miata – the original car won several awards and accolades before it went on sale as well.

"Since its introduction in 1989, Mazda has sold more than 450,000 Miatas worldwide, with more than half of that total coming in North America. The Miata is the best-selling two-seat roadster in the world. In addition, the Mazda Miata is a champion on the track, earning several SCCA Class championships."

As with the previous generation car, Mazda's marketing people bombarded journalists with press releases about the new model in a bid to get that extra column inch, but the underlying message was usually the same: "Despite all of the changes to the 1999 Mazda Miata, it remains true to its original concept – a lightweight, affordable, two-seat roadster that delivers the pure enjoyment of wind-in-the-hair driving. It lifts your spirit and renews your soul."

America had only the 1.8-litre car. With a 9.5:1 compression ratio, it was rated at 140bhp at 6500rpm (or 138bhp in California), and had a maximum torque output of 119lbft at 5500rpm (vehicles for California developed 2lbft less, but at a more useful 5000rpm).

The base model had a five-speed manual gearbox, rack-and-pinion steering without power assistance, and 185/60 HR14 tyres mounted on 5.5J x 14 pressed steel

Beautiful publicity shot of the new Roadster, dated January 1998.

This picture of the VS grade was actually used in the first Japanese catalogue.

wheels. All cars came with dual airbags as standard and – amazingly – a combined stereo radio/CD player with a digital clock. Basic options included air conditioning, power steering, automatic transmission (not available with the Sports Package), a detachable hard-top, foglights, and bright wheel trim rings. However, there were now no fewer than five option packages to choose from:

Touring Package: This added power-assisted steering, 6J x 14 alloy wheels, power windows and mirrors, and a Nardi three-spoke, leather-trimmed steering wheel. Automatic transmission became an option with this package.

Popular Equipment Package: This included the items in the Touring Package, plus a Torsen lsd (on manual cars), cruise control, power door locks, an upgraded sound system, electric aerial, and the patented Windblocker. ABS brakes became an option if the Bose stereo system was purchased at the same time.

Leather Package: Based on the Popular Equipment Package but with the added bonus of a tan leather interior and tan coloured hood, 195/50 VR15 Michelin Pilot SX GT tyres mounted on 6J x 15 alloy rims, plus the high powered Bose stereo radio/cassette/CD unit with top quality speakers. ABS brakes were optional.

Sports Package: This came with manual cars only, and

The official body kit offered by Mazda dealers in Japan at the time of the new model's launch.

The engine of the 1.8-litre RS grade. With a 9.5:1 compression ratio, the 1.8-litre engine produced 145bhp at 6500rpm, and 120lbft of torque at 5000rpm. Note the brace bar, standard on the RS, and optional on the other models. The RS also came with an uprated suspension package, including Bilstein dampers.

American advertising from early 1998. Note the airdam at the front and the side skirts, meaning that the car used in the picture was fitted with the optional Appearance Package.

included a Torsen lsd, 15-inch alloys with the 195/50 tyres, a three-spoke Nardi leather-wrapped steering wheel, an uprated suspension (including Bilstein shock absorbers), a front strut tower brace, front airdam, and rear spoiler.

Appearance Package: The Appearance Package was not available with the Sports Package, but included a front airdam, side skirts, a rear spoiler, rear mudflaps, and foglights.

Standard colours included White, Brilliant Black, Classic Red, Twilight Blue Mica, Highlight Silver Metallic and Emerald Mica. Trim was in black cloth, or tan leather via the aforementioned package, although the latter was not available with the Sports Package. Prices started at $19,770, which was only around $100 different to the cost of the old car.

The cover from the Detroit Show press release. The matching photograph contained within it had a caption that read: "The 1999 Miata is proof that the sequel can be better than the original. Featuring a dramatically restyled body, improved handling, a glass rear window with defroster and an increase in horsepower to 140, the all-new Miata is ready to continue its reign as the best-selling two-seat roadster in the world." This car features the 15-inch alloys that came as part of the Leather Package.

A rear view of the 1999 MX-5 Miata for the American market. Note the optional five-spoke alloy wheels: these being the 14-inch versions, although the 15-inch items looked very similar.

The new car in Europe

The second generation MX-5 made its European debut at the 1998 Geneva Show, held from 5 to 15 March. In his opening statement at the Swiss event, James E Miller said: "I am delighted to welcome you to the Geneva Motor Show for the first time as President of the Mazda Motor Corporation. Mazda has earned an excellent reputation for superior design and engineering capabilities – a reputation that reflects its attention to form, functionality and advanced technology, as well as its emphasis on creativity and craftsmanship.

The 1.8-litre BP-ZE (RS) engine that powered the US range – the 1.6 unit was not listed in America. Rated at 140bhp in most States, cars destined for California, New York, Massachusetts and Connecticut lost 2bhp because of tighter emissions regulations.

Interior of the standard Miata, showing the Nardi steering wheel supplied as part of the Touring Package (and therefore the Leather, and Popular Equipment Packages), and the Sports Package – the base model had a four-spoke, urethane-covered wheel. Again, however, American cars had to do without the option of a wood-rimmed wheel. Interestingly, the Windblocker was not fitted on standard base models, or those equipped with the Touring Package or Sports Package.

The Leather Package's stylish cockpit. Seat facings were trimmed in tan leather, with the rest finished in a matching vinyl. In America, the passenger airbag could actually be deactivated to allow a child seat to be used.

The Miata where it belongs – on the open road.

A confusing photograph of the British 1.6i – confusing because this car is fitted with 14-inch alloys instead of the 15-inch items that are listed as optional in the specifications sheet. The 14-inch wheels would usually be supplied as a £440 option through dealerships, thus allowing owners to keep their original tyres, whereas the move to larger alloys naturally demanded new rubber as well. The 1.6i was launched with a list price of £15,520.

One of the pictures that came with the Geneva Show press pack. Although the MX-5 was an important car for enthusiasts, Mazda gave almost as much attention to the 626 and the various concept cars that had made their debut almost five months earlier in Tokyo.

Interior of the 1.8iS, with a Nardi three-spoke steering wheel. The Windblocker can clearly be seen in this picture, folded down behind the seats. On colder days, it can be raised to an upright position, thus stopping chilly drafts in the cockpit.

The 1.8iS was the UK's top model, priced at £18,775. It came with 6J x 15 alloys and a host of extras as standard, but the detachable hard-top was still a pricey option at £1475.

A right-hand drive press car running on steel rims.

Various publicity shots of the MX-5 for mainland Europe, this particular car sporting 14-inch alloys. Each EU market seemed to select its own specification.

The 1.6-litre engine used in a lot of European markets.

Another European (lhd) specification MX-5, with views of the cars's nose, interior, and tail. The latter picture shows the hood fully erected, giving us a view of the new glass rear window, along with the latest rear light design which eliminated the need for a seperate foglight.

NEW ROADSTER
TOURING
KIT A-spec.

スポーツカーの
正統なる進化。

新型ロードスター用
「ツーリングキット A-スペック」
新発売！

もう20年以上も世界のサーキットで戦ってきた我々でさえ、
新型ロードスターをチューニングすることは、
チューナー冥利につきる魅力的な作業といえる。
なぜならこの車は、先代が持つライトウェイトスポーツの
基本理念をかたくなに踏襲した、まさに「走るため」だけに
生まれた純粋な「スポーツカー」そのものであるからだ。
この「スポーツカー」を際限なくチューニングすれば、
やがて一般公道を走行できない「レーシングカー」になってしまう。
が、しかし少しでもそれに近づけたい。
そんな想いから「ツーリングキットA-スペック」は誕生した。
開発にはもちろんレーシングカーと同様の手法を踏んでいる。
綿密な風洞実験、度重なる走行テスト、膨大なデータ解析等々…。
全身にレーシングカー譲りの機能パーツをまとった
この車のステアリングを握った瞬間から、
スポーツカーの正統な進化を体感できるはずだ。

＊写真の車のステッカーは撮影用です。
商品には含まれておりません。

MAZDASPEED

*Mazdaspeed's Touring Kit A-Spec
for the new Roadster, announced in February 1998, a month after
sales of the second generation model started in Japan.*

Japanese advertising from the spring of 1998.

Another shot of the MX-5 in action, but this is a UK specification 1.8iS. Sales started on 25 April in the British Isles.

"Today Mazda exhibits automobiles that exemplify our new approach based on this long-standing tradition: the all-new MX-5, the new 626 Station Wagon and the Demio Concept along with the MV-X and SW-X concept cars. The new MX-5 will be marketed in Europe starting in April. The redesign features heightened response and power for truly fun sports car driving, yet retains the feeling of oneness between car and driver that MX-5 users have come to expect and love. We hope that you will feel the strength of our enthusiasm for the future of automobiles through the cars and technology you will see at this show."

The press pack highlighted the following points:

Compact, fun-to-drive package
The optimum product package, balanced for driving pleasure. Mazda made extra efforts to minimize the vehicle weight of the new MX-5. Decreasing both front and rear overhang weight and placing all the mass as close to the vehicle centre as possible, enabled the new MX-5 to achieve excellent yaw inertia moment and ideal weight destribution.

More sporty look and feel
The body is attractive from all angles and retains the MX-5's distinctive design motif. Its sporty look is enhanced by lines that stress the wide and low form. Inside, the cockpit is simple and more functional.

Excellent driving pleasure
The new MX-5 offers sharply enhanced driving performance when compared with the original MX-5, thanks to the powerful 1.8-litre and 1.6-litre in-line four-cylinder dohc 16v engine, and excellent driving stability, made possible by a highly-rigid body and chassis. The five-speed manual transmission further enhances the fun of sports driving.

Superb safety features
The new Mazda MX-5 offers excellent active safety features to help prevent accidents, and outstanding passive safety features to help protect the driver and the passenger in the event of an accident.

Improved functionality
The new MX-5 delivers enhanced practicality with more convenient and comfort-enhancing functions and features. [With new packaging, it offers 42 per cent more luggage space.]

The UK press launch was held on the French Riviera, with the car going on sale to the public from the end of April. Special music, *The Song of the Swift* by John Harle, was played at the dealerships, and tape cassettes of the tune were given as gifts in boxes finished in the same gold colour as seen on the new MX-5.

As the UK press release stated: "The new Mazda MX-5 offers enhanced performance and excellent handling and stability. The 0-62mph [100kph] acceleration time for the 1.6-litre is now just 9.7 seconds, a reduction of 0.9 seconds. The 1.8-litre reaches 0-62mph in 8.0 seconds, down 0.7 seconds from the previous car. Top speed for the 1.6-litre is now 118mph (189kph) - up 9mph, or 14kph - and 127mph (203kph) - up 4mph, or 6kph – for the 1.8-litre.

"The 1.6-litre has had power increased by 20bhp (from 90bhp to 110bhp). The 1.8-litre is up 9bhp (from 131bhp to 140bhp). Output and torque for both engines has been improved through enhancements to the intake and exhaust systems, resulting in smooth engine revving from low to high speeds and responsive acceleration."

Indeed, in European trim, with a 9.4:1 compression ratio, the 1.6-litre engine produced 110bhp at 6500rpm, and 99lbft of torque at 5000rpm. On the 1.8, which had a 9.5:1 compression ratio, power was quoted at 140bhp at 6500rpm, while maximum torque output was listed as 119lbft at 4500rpm.

All of the new MX-5s were sold with power steering, an immobilizer, and airbags for both driver and passenger as standard; steel 5.5J x 14 wheels were the norm, fitted with 185/60 HR14 tyres. The 1.8-litre model added electric windows and a Windblocker to the basic specification, while the 1.8iS also came with 195/50 VR15 tyres mounted on 6J x 15 alloys and a number of other more upmarket touches – ABS braking, a Torsen lsd, electrically adjusted door mirrors, power door locks, a stereo radio/cassette with electric aerial, mudflaps, and stainless treadplates. In addition, a Nardi leather-trimmed steering wheel replaced the urethane-covered item.

In Britain, the 1.6i was listed at £15,520 on the road (almost £1000 more than its predecessor, or about the price of the old 1.8i); the new 1.8i was priced at £16,650, while the 1.8iS was little changed at £18,775. Major options included air conditioning, a detachable hard-top, front foglamps, and a rear spoiler. The Windblocker, alloy wheels, stainless treadplates, and front and rear mudflaps were also made available to upgrade cheaper models.

Standard colours included Classic Red, Classic Black, Racing Silver Metallic, Racing Blue Mica, Racing Green Mica and Racing Bronze Mica, although the metallic and mica shades added £250 to the price of the car. The upholstery was usually in black cloth, but leather could be specified as a £923 option, the colour choices being black, light grey, anthracite, tan, taupe and mist.

It's interesting to note that automatic transmission was not listed anywhere in Europe. Some European mainland countries, however, such as Italy, got the 15-inch alloy wheels as standard on both the 1.6 and 1.8-litre models, although the ABS braking system,

Torsen limited-slip differential, and Nardi steering wheel were reserved for the larger engined car.

Switzerland had two 1.6-litre grades (the 1.6 Youngster and 1.6 SE Youngster), and one 1.8 – the 1.8 Youngster. The basic 1.6 came with steel wheels and a traditional braking system, but the other grades had 15-inch alloys and ABS as standard. Only the 1.8 was fitted with the Torsen lsd, however. Overall weights on European cars ranged from 1015kg (2233lb) for the basic 1.6, to 1047kg (2303lb) for the UK spec 1.8iS.

Mazdaspeed

As Mazda's representative in the field of motorsport and the factory's outlet for works tuning parts, it's not surprising that Mazdaspeed was the first company to offer aerodynamic body kits and tuning components. In a news release, the Touring Kit A-Spec was announced as follows: "Mazdaspeed Co. Ltd is proud to announce that the Touring Kit A-Spec for the new Roadster (NB8C/NB6C) is now under development and will be available through its Sport Factory, other nationwide Mazda group dealers and retailers from 26 February 1998.

"The development of the Touring Kit A-Spec has been made on the orthodox and evolutionary concept focusing on the aerodynamic and suspension parts to withdraw maximum onroad potential. A special feature of the tuning parts is the overall three-dimensional body design with which wind tunnel tests showed a positive improvement to the Cd (the air resistance factor) and Cl (the lift factor) readings. In addition, the front spoiler is that of the first generation Air Scoop design reducing air resistance. Furthermore, the headlight finisher has been designed to provide a smooth look with a strong outline definition. Moreover, the three-dimensional shaped side skirt allows the airflow to channel smoothly by the body side. All other aero-parts, namely the rear wing and rear skirt, have undergone wind tunnel tests to find their optimum setting to increase the aerodynamic effect.

"Optional parts designed for the new Roadster (MX-5) include a newly-designed air filter. This adopts three special layered Welten Sponges which in tests showed a suction restriction of 20 per cent, contributing to better fuel economy and accelerator response. Secondly, [for the 1.8-litre car, there is a] limited-slip differential which has been designed for better traction for both wheels, enabling controlled and effective cornering.

"An additional item [for the 1.8-litre model] is the asbestos-free brake set designed for durability and controllability. The clutch set has been designed to transmit high power from the engine to the drivetrain. Furthermore, a lighter flywheel is available, enabling a quick engine response without engine stall or difficult clutch operation. A shaving process of the chrome-molybdenum and the ion-nitrogen treatment has been

carried out on the flywheel surface, making this product a sufficiently hard and durable item.

"Moreover, suspension parts, sports sound muffler, exhaust manifold, roll bar, sports driving meters [white-faced gauges], high volt silicone leads, and the brake line set are presently undergoing development and will be available from April.

"Among the selections of Touring kit devised for public roads is the Touring Kit A-Spec, of which, parts exclusively for competition use are called the Sports Kit. Each part can be purchased separately to tailor the needs and budget of the buyer."

Prices ranged from 35,000 yen for the headlight finishers, up to 58,000 yen for a rear spoiler or the side skirts. The body kit was completed by the front spoiler and rear skirt, each priced at 48,000 yen. Mazdaspeed seats ranged from 64,000 to 88,000 yen apiece.

Mechanical components for the 1.8-litre car included the limited-slip differential at 75,000 yen, and the front pad set at 15,000 yen (2000 yen more than for the rear set). For both power units, 48,000 yen would buy the lightened flywheel, while the clutch set was 54,000 yen on the 1.8, or 52,000 on the 1.6-litre.

Initial press reaction

In America, *Motor Trend* was very quick to cover the new model, claiming that "although the second generation of this petite two-seater rolls onto the scene next spring with a new look and new level of sophistication, remaining fully intact are all the wonderful traits that made the original car fun to drive and easy to own." This view was echoed in *Road & Track*, the sub-heading of its April 1998 test reading: "The same basic formula taken to new heights."

Thos L Bryant introduced the car to Australian readers in *Wheels* magazine, and had this to say: "The tail of the MX-5 prototype wiggled just a little as I went through a series of esses at the Miyoshi Proving Ground. The signal from the car was polite but firm: 'You're going too fast for these conditions.' As I eased off and the all-new MX-5 settled itself, a grin spread across my face. I've loved the MX-5 since it was introduced in 1989, but this new one is markedly improved."

Writing for the popular British *Top Gear* magazine in February 1998, Yasushi Ishiwatari noted: "Though it's not exactly a quantum leap in styling from the old MX-5, there's more to be enthusiastic about than you'd think; it really does feel more like a new car than anyone would imagine from looking at it ... It hasn't lost any of the charm of its predecessor. The good points have been further improved, and they've fixed many of the niggly and irritating problems."

The same journal carried out a comparison test between the MX-5 1.8iS, MGF and Fiat Barchetta. Although it felt the new car was not as much fun as the original, and had lost some of its character along the way, the Mazda still came out on top.

In a similar test, *Car* thought it was an obvious decision in favour of the car from Hiroshima: "Compared with the Mazda, the Barchetta is too much the fashion model and not enough the mean mover, while the MGF is the victim of a purge against its dynamic purity. It's also too expensive. That's an accusation you can't level at the lovable Barchetta, but the Mazda has to be worth the extra outlay for its driving entertainment. Or you can have an MX-5 1.6 for Barchetta money – and there's also the question of whether you could live with the Fiat's compulsory left-hand drive layout.

"Whenever we've tested 'affordable' sports cars recently, the result has never been clear-cut. This time, with just a slight confusion in the styling plot, it's simple. Mazda's new MX-5 does all that a sports car should. It's a cracker."

Autocar (which added BMW's Z3, launched in time for the 1997 season, to the equation) was also wooed by the appeal of the MX-5. In its verdict on the new 1.8-litre MX-5, *Autocar* said in another article: "[It has a] much improved chassis [and] better quality interior materials make the cabin more classy. Mazda's jewel finely polished."

As you will have gathered, almost all of the early road tests were complimentary, and Mazda was often praised for not making changes for the sake of it. The Japanese *Motor Magazine* seemed to sum up the mood perfectly: "The new car is the next level up from the first generation Eunos Roadster. The looks have changed, but the soul remains the same."

After an uncertain start, the original MX-5 went on to take the world by storm. If initial reactions were anything to go by, the future looked set to be every bit as good as the past had been for Mazda's LWS ...

Chapter 4

THE LEGEND CONTINUES

Following a successful launch, the Mazda team now had the difficult task of selling the second generation model. Sports cars were falling from favour with the young and trendy – they were not as fashionable as RVs and SUVs, and insurance premiums on sporty two-door machines had escalated to such an extent that many potential buyers were put off the idea upon discovering how much it would cost to insure the vehicle. Yet more and more manufacturers were entering the LWS arena all the time.

At the 1995 Tokyo Show, Toyota exhibited the MRJ, which was later developed into the MR-S concept of 1997. Although slow to join the LWS class, Toyota's intentions were clear. The MR-S (also known as the MR2 Roadster and MR2 Spyder) duly went on sale at the end of 1999 on the home market, with export sales beginning in April 2000. Another debutante at the 1995 Tokyo Show was the Honda SSM, which later became the superb S2000 production model of 1999 vintage. Mitsubishi also joined the open sports car fold with its Eclipse Spyder (recently heavily revised for the 2001 model year), and there were even rumours of Isuzu building a two-seater, only to be quashed when the company announced its withdrawal from all but the RV and commercial vehicle arena.

On the European front, Audi showed its TT Coupé at the 1995 Frankfurt Show, and followed it up with a Roadster version for the Japanese event. The TT Roadster would also go into production, joining the likes of the MGF, Fiat Barchetta, Alfa Romeo Spider, BMW Z3, the Lotus Elise and Caterham 21 (both of these Brits were announced at the 1995 Earls Court Show, but deliveries would not start until late 1996), and the Mercedes-Benz SLK (eventually launched in time for the 1997 model year after a protracted arrival) for a bite of the open sports car market. There was also the Porsche Boxster, though it's fair to say that price probably elevated it to a slightly different level.

From America, perhaps only the well established Ford Mustang and Chevrolet Camaro convertibles could

The author's wife, Miho, fell in love with this 1.6-litre Roadster we hired during a trip to Okinawa in December 1998. We've owned two NB2s since.

Tail of the 1999 Miata.

be classed as true competitors. However, there was no doubt that the MX-5 had a great deal of new competition to contend with in a shrinking market ...

The 1999 season in Japan

There was little change in the home market line-up for 1999; even the catalogue was the same as that for the previous season. However, the 1.6-litre five-speed basic model was now priced at 1,770,000 yen (although deleting the standard air conditioning brought it down to 1,594,000 yen), the M Package was listed at 1,860,000 yen (or 2,003,000 yen with automatic transmission), while the Special Package was 1,960,000 yen in manual guise, or 98,000 yen more if the buyer wanted an automatic gearbox.

In the 1.8-litre line-up, the entry level S grade cost 2,185,000 yen with a six-speed manual transmission, or 2,233,000 yen with an automatic. The manual only RS was listed at 2,295,000 yen, whilst the top-of-the-range VS came in at 2,395,000 yen, or 2,443,000 yen as an automatic. All of these prices were held until the start of the 2000 model year.

America's 1999 model year proper

Although the second generation was known as a 1999 model from the time of its launch, the 1999 model year proper was announced in September 1998. Naturally,

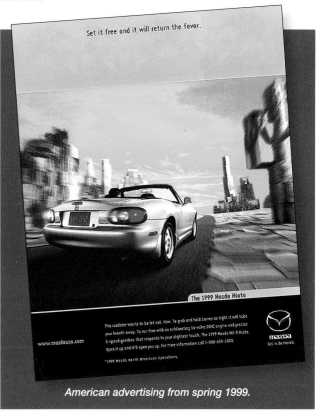

American advertising from spring 1999.

changes were few – even the $19,770 sticker price was carried over.

Essentially, the option packages were much the same, too. For the 1999 season, the Touring Package was priced at $1100, the Popular Equipment Package was $2330 (or $1940 with automatic models, as the Torsen lsd was not supplied), the Leather Package was $3975 (again, it was $390 cheaper on automatic cars because of the lack of a limited-slip differential), while the Sports Package was $1900.

One of the few changes made was in the Appearance Package, which now came in two parts. The front airdam, side skirts and rear mudguards were batched together at $595 (code 1AP), while the full set – everything in 1AP, plus a rear spoiler and foglights – came in at $995. Not surprisingly, this was given the 2AP moniker. In addition, there was a Power Steering Package which included PAS and wheel trim rings only.

Individual options included air conditioning ($900), power-assisted steering ($300), automatic transmission ($850), ABS brakes ($550 when combined with certain packages), a detachable hard-top ($1500), foglights ($250), front and rear mudguards ($125), the Bose stereo upgrade ($550), a cassette player ($250), wheel trim rings ($50), and floormats at $80; the patented Windblocker was available with the Touring or Sports Package for an extra $150.

Advertising from the Auto Exe concern of Tokyo, and featuring the new Roadster. The gentleman at the top of the page is Japan's very own "Mr Le Mans" – Yojiro Terada. The founder of Auto Exe, Terada's links with the Mazda marque extend over four decades.

Accessories

Rear Spoiler, Side Sill Set, Rear Mud Flap Set

Detachable Hard Top and Stainless Steel Door Edge Protector Set

Scuff Plate Set

Front Air Dam Skirt and Fog Lamp Set

Wood Trim Kit, Gear Knob and Parking Brake Grip

Rear Wing Spoiler

Full Tonneau Cover

Luggage Carrier

14" Image Alloy Wheels

Radio Cassette - CD Autochanger Compatible

Radio - Single CD - CD Changer Compatible

6 Disc Autochanger

14" Stealth Alloy Wheels

15" Reflex Alloy Wheels

15" Gemini Alloy Wheels

Some of the accessories offered by Mazda UK for the 1999 season. Note that all of the components which came together to make the MX-5 Sport were available as separate dealer options.

The 1999 MY Miata fitted with the Leather and Appearance Packages. A total of 25,332 MX-5s had been shipped to North America in 1998 (just under 1300 of which went to Canada), although the figure dropped to 16,763 units the following year (15,591 for the USA; 1172 for Canada).

European update

In Britain, prices and options on the three original MX-5 grades were carried over for the 1999 model year, so the 1.6i was listed at £15,520, the 1.8i was £16,650, and 1.8iS was £18,775. At the end of 1998, however, these were joined by a new model – the MX-5 Sport.

The MX-5 Sport was based on the 1.8iS, but had a number of extras as standard. It came with air conditioning, a detachable hard-top finished in body colour, leather trim (all previously expensive options), along with the body styling kit (including a lowered front airdam with foglights, side skirts, rear mudflaps and a rear spoiler) and wood trim kit that were usually offered as accessories.

Indeed, Mazda UK had an extensive list of dealer options. As well as the aforementioned items (the wood trim kit consisted of a console finishing piece, gearknob and handbrake grip, incidentally), dealerships were able to offer various alloy wheel designs, a radio/cassette or radio with a built-in, single-play CD, a CD autochanger, stainless treadplates, door edge protectors, a tonneau cover, and a rear deck luggage rack. Incidentally, during the 1998 calendar year, Mazda sold a total of 6307 MX-5s in the British Isles, while sales for the rest of Europe amounted to around 15,000 units for the same period.

The 10th Anniversary model

Just in time for the 1999 season, the 1.8-litre Roadster 10th Anniversary model was launched. The equipment specification was basically the same for all markets around the world, with 7500 being produced in total. Japan was allocated 500 of these, at a price of 2,483,000 yen. To put that into perspective, the new RX-7 range started at 2,898,000 yen at the time.

Features included a six-speed manual transmission, polished 15-inch alloys, an uprated suspension with Bilstein shock absorbers (to Japanese RS specifications), air conditioning, dual airbags, half-leather, two-tone trim (with a matching steering wheel and gearknob), a Bose CD sound system surrounded by a carbonfibre-style console trim, chrome rings around the gauges, central locking, unique treadplates and floormats, a blue hood, and a striking Innocent Blue Mica paint finish; each came with a certificate of authenticity, special badging (which carried the car's number) and a commemorative ignition key.

Of the 7500 produced, 3700 were destined for Europe, and Britain received 600 of them, priced at £21,100 apiece. Like the Japanese market model, it featured Innocent Blue Mica coachwork, a two-tone black and blue interior, a blue soft-top and hood cover, and the six-speed gearbox - the first time the latter had been offered outside Japan; the UK model also came with ABS brakes.

Top Gear looked at the limited edition vehicle in its May 1999 issue. Tom Stewart said: "The standard MX-5 already pretty much sets the standard for pin-sharp,
(continued on page 70)

This is the 10th Anniversary model that Top Gear tested. The magazine was full of praise for this latest variation, but only 600 of them were available in Britain (sales starting from 3 April). Note the tiny badge on the trailing edge of the front wing – it stated the car's limited edition number, and always appeared on the driver's side.

The 10th Anniversary car had black leather seats with blue suede-like inserts, and a steering wheel and gearlever to match. It came with red needles on the gauges, like all six-speed models in Japan since the launch of the second generation. Of course, for the Americans and Europeans, this was something new, as the limited edition vehicle marked the debut of the six-speed gearbox in those markets. Note also the carbonfibre-style console trim.

A British brochure for the 10th Anniversary limited edition.

Cover from the Mazda UK model range brochure for the 1999 model range. It featured the MX-5 Sport - a new variant, taking the British line-up to four MX-5 models.

The 500,000th MX-5, pictured in the Mazda Museum. Built for the American market, it was finished in Evolution Orange Mica, a colour that wasn't officially available in the States until the 2000 model year.

was built – a US specification model finished in Evolution Orange Mica with a leather interior. This was an important landmark in the MX-5's history, prompting a special ceremony at the Ujina factory.

The home market & the NR Limited

There was very little change for the 2000 model year in Japan, although prices increased slightly – by the princely sum of 20,000 yen on all grades – from 1 October 1999. It was hardly a figure to worry about, and perhaps gave as good an indication as any of how competitive this sector of the market had become.

During December 1999, Mazda announced the NR Limited. Based on the manual 1.8-litre S grade, it featured Art Vin Red Mica bodywork, a parchment coloured leather interior with matching beige hood, polished 15-inch alloy wheels (they were the familiar five-spoke 6J x 15 rims, but buffed to look like those on the 10th Anniversary model), a front tower brace in body colour, and a few items borrowed from the VS, including the Bose stereo radio/CD unit, wood-rimmed Nardi steering wheel (plus the wooden gearknob and handbrake trim, all in a slightly darker material than usual), stainless treadplates, and remote central locking. A unique feature was the meter panel, which incorporated white-faced gauges with chrome finishing rings – definitely a glimpse into the future – and there was also fake wood trim on the centre console.

Limited to just 500 examples, the NR Limited was priced at 2,516,000 yen, or 2,566,000 yen with floormats

balanced handling, but subtle chassis improvements on this model further improve the car's already accurate steering and superb cornering prowess. The firmer Bilsteins haven't eradicated the MX-5's slight skittishness over the bumps when pushed, but the car's still a hoot on a twisty road and the new six-speed 'box makes a big contribution. Use it properly and the motor will never be caught off guard."

America received 3150 of these special six-speed vehicles (where the colour was known as Sapphire Blue), and Australia took the remaining 150. Whereas home market sales began at the beginning of January 1999, export deliveries started during the spring. As in Japan, buyers were treated to a pair of blue-faced wristwatches.

Incidentally, on 8 February 1999, the 500,000th car

Japan's elegant NR Limited. A similar six-speed model was duly launched in Europe and the States, although all had subtle differences.

Interior of the NR Limited. Note the white faces on the gauges and the darker than usual wood on the steering wheel, gearknob and handbrake grip. All 500 cars had a six-speed transmission, as an automatic was not offered.

This was the only Roadster on display at the 1999 Tokyo Show. It was joined by an RX-7 finished in the same colour, but it was the RX-EVOLV concept car that received most of the crowd's attention. This rotary-engined machine was later developed into the RX-8.

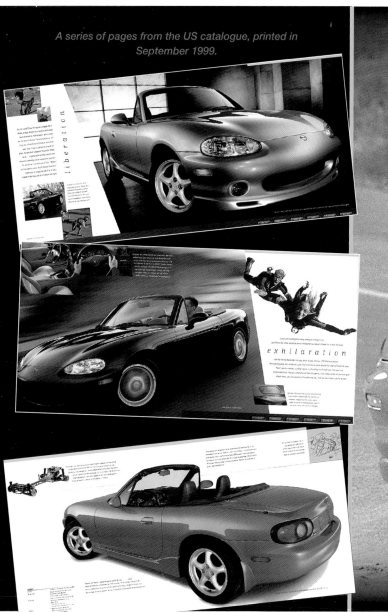

A series of pages from the US catalogue, printed in September 1999.

and other necessities. Sales started from 18 January, and officially, no options were offered with the vehicle.

Car Graphic compared the sporty 1800RS with the Toyota MR-S in its January 2000 issue. It declared that the Toyota was great fun and dynamically hard to fault. However, as a long-term prospect, it would plump for the Mazda – no less a sports car, but with a distinct advantage in the practicality stakes. It was also felt to be the more attractive of the two, although, in all fairness, the author has noticed that an awful lot depends on the coachwork colour.

Cover from the American brochure for the 2000 model year Miata.

Y2K in America

The 2000 model year saw an extensive reshuffle in the Miata line. The base model continued, acquiring alloy wheels shod with 185/60 HR14 rubber, power-assisted steering, the exclusive three-spoke, leather-trimmed Nardi steering wheel, electrically adjusted door mirrors, power windows and an automatic aerial along the way, but it was now joined by an 'LS' grade.

The LS came with five-spoke 15-inch alloys, slightly wider, VR-rated tyres, a Torsen lsd, cruise control, the 200W Bose stereo system (with a cassette deck added as well), a tan leather interior and tan coloured soft-top,

the Windblocker, power door locks, and floormats. ABS brakes were available as an option on this model.

Naturally, with the higher standard specifications, increases in both weight and price could be expected – and there were. The base model was now 15kg (33lb) heavier at 1060kg (2332lb) and $21,245, while the new LS grade was 1082kg (2381lb) and $23,995.

In line with the revisions, the options were also changed. The base model could be upgraded via the Convenience Package (with cruise control, central locking, the Windblocker, and two additional door-mounted speakers) for $795, or with the $995 Suspension Package

The 2000 Miata Special Edition – America's NR Limited.

– but not both. The Suspension Package came with an uprated suspension, a front strut brace, Torsen lsd, and 15-inch alloy wheels. It was also available on the LS, but with the limited-slip differential and larger alloys already part of the standard specification, it was only $495 on that vehicle.

The 1AP Appearance Package continued unchanged, but the 2AP option was deleted from the lists. Instead, the rear spoiler and foglights were priced individually, at $295 and $250 respectively. Other options included air conditioning ($900), automatic transmission ($900), ABS brakes ($550), a hard-top ($1500), mudguards ($125) and, for the base model, a Torsen lsd ($395), cassette deck ($250), the Windblocker ($150), and floormats, quoted at $80.

Dealers were also able to provide such goodies as a front mask (or 'bra' as it is affectionately known in the States), a tonneau cover, treadplates, a wooden dash

The little Mazda sports car continued to be as popular as ever in the UK.

74

Mark Fields – Mazda's new President – seen here with an RX-8 styling model.

kit, wooden gearknob, a chrome rear deck rack, and a purpose-made car cover.

In addition, at last, the signature gold bodywork colour – seen everywhere at the time of the second generation model's launch – was made available in the States, known in this market as Evolution Orange Mica. The other six coachwork colours continued unchanged, with black cloth for the interior on the base car, and tan leather for the LS. The hood was the same shade as the interior trim in all cases.

Peter Nunn compared a Miata LS with the new Toyota MR2 Spyder for *Automobile* magazine and concluded: "The Toyota puts up a good fight and is the value winner here. It's the more eco-friendly roadster, one that's strong on refinement, quality, and the ability to cover ground effortlessly. It's new and it's different, but the design is peculiar and space utilization is poor. As it has been since day one, the Miata is something special – to look at, to sit in, to drive, and to own. After two days of hard driving, the decision between the new Toyota and the Mazda was an easy one to make. The Miata is still magic."

At *Car & Driver*, too, the Miata won the battle, although only just on this occasion. Described as "the Japanese roadster with more soul than James Brown," it was the car's styling and distinct advantage in the practicality stakes that handed the victory to the Mazda.

In all fairness, though, when *Road & Track* brought the two Japanese competitors together, it was a different story: Dennis Simanaitis (a long-term Miata owner) went for the MR2, while Douglas Kott voted for the Hiroshima

machine. Both lapped the Willow Springs race track within a fraction of a second of its rival, and each covered the standing-quarter in similar times (the Mazda in 16.1 seconds, the Toyota in 15.6). They went through the handling tests evenly matched, but the MR2 shone in the braking department. Ultimately, the Toyota won the day on a clear cut points decision, but it was noted: "Both the Miata and MR2 deserve to sell like hotcakes."

From the author's personal experience of the two cars, he would have to agree with that closing statement. After a test drive, one can quickly establish that both are dynamically superb, and both are a lot of fun. In this case, a sale depends not so much on which car is 'better', but on which set of plus and minus points that come with such different designs are the most critical to the buyer.

The British 2000 model year

Prices were increased slightly for the 2000 season, meaning that the 1.6i was listed at £15,685, the 1.8i was £16,815, and the 1.8iS £18,790. In addition to the standard line-up, Mazda UK brought back the SE model, announced in mid-September 1999.

The SE (or MX-5 Special Edition to give it its proper title) was limited to 500 units, priced at £18,495 apiece. The 1.8-litre model came with Racing Green coachwork, a tan leather interior and matching hood, 15-inch alloys, power-assisted steering with a Nardi wood-rimmed wheel (complemented by a wooden gearknob and centre console trim), and electric windows.

As a matter of interest, Mazda UK sold 6411 MX-5s during the 1999 calendar year – 104 more than the previous annual total. Including those destined for sale in Britain, no fewer than 23,255 vehicles were exported to Europe that year.

Corporate news

The start of 1999 saw a massive shift in exchange rates around the world. The introduction of the ECU in Europe led to the pound weakening against the yen, as Japan threw its support behind the new currency. From a peak of 240 yen to £1 in the autumn of 1998, the rate settled back to around 200 before moving quickly to 185 yen to £1 in the opening days of the new year.

However, despite the unfavourable rates, by 1999, after six fiscal years of recording an operational loss, Mazda was once again profitable. Good results in Europe had a lot to do with this turnaround in fortune: figures released for January-June 1999 revealed MX-5 sales of 13,448 units – up 70 per cent on the same period in 1998.

December 1999 saw another change at the top, with Mark Fields taking over the reins from James Miller as Mazda's President. Born in 1961, Fields joined Ford in 1989, and quickly moved up the ranks. A real car enthusiast, he first became attached to the Mazda marque in 1998. In an enlightening interview for the RJC, Fields revealed his plans to reduce the time involved between a design-freeze and a new model entering production (which bodes well for some of Mazda's interesting prototypes unveiled recently), and his desire to allow the company to move in a uniquely Mazda direction – to encourage the engineers, designers and management to let Mazda's spirit and flair show in its products, rather than try and follow others in the chase for mainstream sales. It's a refreshing viewpoint, and one that the author supports wholeheartedly.

The Miata Mono-Posto

We'd seen the Club Racer, the M-Speedster and the M-Coupé based on the first generation model, but few were prepared for the Miata Mono-Posto Concept that appeared at the 2000 Los Angeles Show, although those attending the 1999 SEMA Show for aftermarket tuning had already been given a sneak preview.

Inspired by the legendary road racers of the 1950s, Tom Matano stated: "It has been designed for someone who prefers to be alone with the road, focused purely on driving." With only one seat (the meaning of monoposto), the driver didn't have much choice but to be alone! This was a pure driving machine: with a 190bhp turbocharged engine (the extra power and torque – all 243lbft of it – coming courtesy of HKS, the tuning specialist), wide, 18-inch wheels and tyres, and uprated braking and suspension, it was much more than just a styling exercise.

Finished in a striking Red Pearl Mica, the Mono-Posto Concept certainly attracted attention. The engine was modified to produce 190bhp at 6100rpm, with maximum torque quoted as 243lbft at 4100rpm. It was estimated that 0-60 could be covered in around six seconds!

The Miata Mono-Posto Concept that made its debut at the 2000 Los Angeles Show.

Interior of the Mono-Posto Concept.

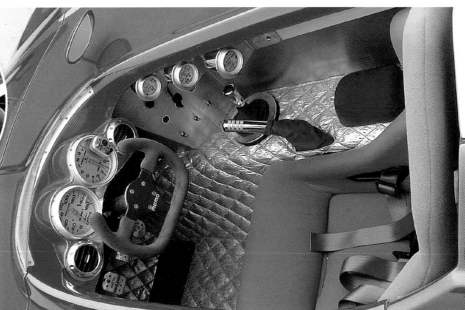

A press photograph of the MX-5 Jasper Conran Platinum. The Platinum title derives from the name of the car's unique paint. With this in mind, the Classic Black title needs no explanation. Only 100 were finished in this silver colour, with 400 in black.

Conran and the MX-5 limited edition that carried his name.

The New Mazda MX-5 Jasper Conran 100. Limited edition.
Look hard and you might find one. 0345 48 48 48

Limited to only 100, features include unique Platinum panel, Red Connolly leather seats and red carpets, aluminium effect interior, BBS alloy wheels and state-of-the-art Sony CD and minidisc autochanger system.
The Mazda MX-5 Jasper Conran also comes in Classic Black with Black Connolly leather interior – limited to 400.

Model shown: Mazda MX-5 Jasper Conran 100 limited edition £24,000 on the road. Price includes VAT, number plates, delivery, 12 months' road fund licence and first registration tax. Car shown may not be to exact UK specification – please consult your local Mazda dealer.

mazda
Get in. Be moved.
www.mazda.co.uk

Tasteful advertising for the Jasper Conran model.

The MX-5 Icon was the UK equivalent to the home market NR Limited.

To match the sporting exterior, the cockpit – perhaps the perfect word in this case – was also heavily modified, with a Sparco racing seat, Momo F1-style steering wheel and new instruments providing the finishing touches.

A few months later, the Americans were treated to another special, but this time one they could buy – the 2000 Miata Special Edition. Finished in Mahogany Mica with a parchment coloured leather interior and soft-top, this was basically the US equivalent to the NR Limited. The second Miata to reach American shores with the six-speed transmission (the first had been the 10th Anniversary model), only 3000 were built, priced at $25,055 apiece. In addition to the six-speed gearbox, it came with a Torsen limited-slip differential, polished five-spoke alloy wheels, the Appearance Package, foglights, a Nardi wood-rimmed steering wheel (with a matching gearknob and handbrake handle), white-faced gauges with chrome trim rings, and a top-of-the-range Bose stereo system incorporating a CD player, radio and cassette deck.

British Specials

March 2000 saw the launch of the £19,200 MX-5 Icon. This was basically the same model as Japan's NR Limited and America's Special Edition. As such, it came with a six-speed gearbox, unique Art Vin Red Mica paintwork, an oatmeal coloured leather interior and matching hood, polished 15-inch alloys, white gauges with chrome trim rings, a wood-rimmed Nardi steering wheel and gearknob, plus the standard features one would expect to find on the 1.8iS.

Mazda UK's Managing Director, Tim Tozer, said: "Mazda will only sell 750 Mazda MX-5 Icon models, so owners can add exclusivity to the long list of standard equipment and all the hallmarks of this super sports car. It oozes charm and style, it's fun to drive, and I'm delighted to say that it has already caught the eye of many buyers."

In May, the popular yellow coachwork colour made a welcome return on the MX-5 California. Based on the 1.6-litre model, it featured Sunburst Yellow paint with a black interior, special five-spoke alloy wheels, and a CD player. Only 500 were produced, selling at just £16,000 each – the same as the revised price for the standard 1.6i. By this time, the 1.8i was £17,200, while 1.8iS was quoted as £19,200.

A month later, the MX-5 Jasper Conran made its debut. In reality, this wasn't one limited edition, but two – the 100-off Jasper Conran Platinum and the 400-off Jasper Conran Classic Black. Conran, the famous designer, had the 1.8iS to work on, and gave it a highly distinctive interior. The Platinum version had a unique silver coachwork colour.

The Jasper Conran Platinum carried a red Connolly leather interior (which extended to the door panels and the hood cover) with red carpets – even the boot was trimmed in the same carpet, which played host to a custom-made luggage set on the £24,000 model. Other interior features included an aluminium and leather steering wheel, and aluminium finishes on the centre console, air vents, gearknob, handbrake grip and door pulls.

The Classic Black variant was trimmed in black Connolly hide with black carpets – plus the same unique aluminium pieces – but this £21,000 version lacked the luggage. Both, however, came with a CD/MD stereo system, and 15-inch 12-spoke alloy wheels sourced from the BBS concern.

On 26 July 2000, yet another limited edition model was launched – the MX-5 Isola. This was a 1.6-litre model in Classic Red, but with the added bonus of a body coloured hard-top and five-spoke alloy wheels thrown in for the same price as the standard 1.6i. Only 500 were made available.

Interestingly, despite this flurry of limited edition models, Mazda UK's MX-5 sales fell to 5199 for the year 2000. Although this represented a drop of more than 1200 units on the previous record-breaking season, it should be borne in mind that sales in Britain during the early 1990s were hovering around 20 per cent of this figure. Including those sold in the UK, a total of 19,583 MX-5s were exported to Europe that year.

The MX-5 Isola – yet another limited edition from the UK. It came with a hard-top as part of the package, which is an ideal accessory for coping with British winters. Weighing in at 22kg (48lb), however, it really takes two people to put it on or remove it.

The 1.6-litre MX-5 California, launched in May 2000. Like Britain's 1995 California Limited Edition, it had Sunburst Yellow paintwork, a black interior, and non-standard five-spoke alloys.

Chapter 5

THE NB2 SERIES

In May 2000, the MX-5 was officially recognised in the *Guinness Book of Records* with 'The World's Largest Production of Lightweight Open Two-Seater Sports Car'. However, Mazda was not prepared to rest on its laurels and, on 18 July that year, the Hiroshima concern announced a major face-lift for the Roadster.

The press release read: "Here's good news for lovers of lightweight open two-seater sports cars. The best just got better. Mazda Motor Corporation's new Roadster, just introduced at Mazda Anfini and other selected Mazda dealers throughout Japan, has a powerful new 1.8-litre engine, increased body rigidity, and a number of exterior and interior enhancements.

"Since the launch of the original Roadster in September 1989, Mazda's engineers have continued to embrace the 'Oneness Between Car And Driver' philosophy for the model, aiming at providing drivers with a refreshing feel of open car driving and distinctive styling. Generating a new market for lightweight, open two-seat sports cars, Mazda has sold over 565,000 units of the Roadster worldwide since 1989. The Roadster was recognized recently as the world's top-selling two-seater sports car by Guinness World Records.

"Incorporating a series of significant improvements into the engine, body and suspension system, the new Roadster achieves 'Oneness Between Car And Driver' at an even higher level. Monthly sales volume in Japan is expected to be approximately 500 units.

The release went on to describe the salient points:

New dynamic styling for a sporty, high-grade look
Mazda has revamped the exterior and interior to reflect the company's design theme, 'Contrast In Harmony,' resulting in an even sportier and more forceful look.

The front air intake opening incorporates the 'five-point grille' for the distinctive Mazda family appearance. Slimmer headlamps create a sharp and stylish impression.

The headlamps consist of multi-reflector-type high beam lamps and projector-type low beam lamps. Additionally, the rear combination lamps incorporate a new design that give the turn-flasher compartment a transparent look.

Instrument panel gauges incorporate a white coloured meter panel, a shiny metal frame and an amber illuminated lamp. The re-designed door trims lend a sporty and sophisticated feel.

Opposite page: The face-lifted MX-5, easily distinguished by its new headlights, air intake, and the apertures to each side of it (sometimes used as foglight housings). The latest headlamps on the NB2 are said to be some 20 per cent brighter than those of the original second generation model. Low beam performance is almost as good as main beam with standard halogen lights. Note also the 16-inch wheels and tyres. This is a left-hand drive version for Continental Europe, incidentally.

A word from Takao Kijima (MX-5 Programme Manager) –

At Mazda, when we developed the first generation MX-5, we used the expression 'Oneness Between Car And Driver' for the first time. This expression set the key theme for the MX-5's development, and was expanded to give insight into the driving experience: "Pleasant conversation begins the moment you get in the car, and you forget time as you completely immerse yourself in the enjoyment of driving. The feelings of the driver are precisely communicated to the vehicle as driver and car become one, in a car devoted to having fun throughout the changing seasons."

In developing the second generation MX-5, we set out to express and expand on the many kinds of fun available in the MX-5, with the key theme of 'Lots Of Fun' – the fun of driving a roadster, the fun of manoeuvring a machine, and the fun of owning something with great and timeless styling.

The distinctive individual indentity of the 'Mazda Brand DNA' that distinguishes the marque from our competitors is expressed in three unique personality and product attributes. These personality attributes found in all Mazda cars – 'Stylish', 'Insightful' and 'Spirited' – find expression in the product attributes of 'Distinctive Design,' 'Exceptional Functionality' and 'Responsive Handling And Performance.' This personality is clearly expressed in the MX-5, a model that truly symbolizes the Mazda brand.

To ensure that even more people will come to love the new MX-5, we have made some major changes that further enhance the feeling of 'Oneness Between Car And Driver,' as we set out to take 'Lots Of Fun' to an even higher level. Harnessing recent developments in automotive technology, we have improved the engine, strengthened the body, and fine-tuned the suspension with the aim of achieving the highest possible level of communication between the vehicle and its driver, and a fuller realisation of our 'Lots Of Fun' expression.

We believe that the new MX-5 is a singular car that will stimulate the five senses of its drivers and passengers with its universal appeal. For many people, taking the wheel of the new MX-5 will generate the fun of driving and the fun of manoeuvring a machine. For others, it will bring back the joy of driving, and recollections of their first sports car.

The latest 1.8-litre BP-VE (RS) engine. The S-VT mechanism featured continuous phase variable valve timing to enhance response throughout the rev range. The phase of the intake valve timing to the crank angle is changed continuously in relation to hydraulic pressure by a pen-type actuator, controlled by a computer that calculates the timing. The S-VT system inhibits air intake countercurrents during high load, low rotation periods by closing the intake valve early, to improve low speed torque by increasing charging effiency. Conversely, in high load, high speed situations, the intake valve is closed later, improving output by taking maximum advantage of the inertia of the air being taken in. In medium load operation, the intake valve opens early to expand valve overlap, increasing exhaust gas diffusion and decreasing pumping loss. Maximum power went up to 160bhp, while peak torque output was now 125lbft at 5500rpm.

The 1.6-litre unit continued in a number of markets around the world, but it was not given the benefit of the S-VT mechanism.

The face-lifted interior, with its new gauges, steering wheel design (the three-spoke Nardi wheel was also subtly revised, with the Mazda badge finding its way onto the centre boss), seats, and storage arrangements. This is an automatic 1600M for the Japanese market.

Revisions to the tail-end were more subtle than those at the front of the car, although the new rear combination lights were easy to spot. Again, this is a Japanese-spec vehicle (a 1.6-litre SP), but the same basic design was adopted for all markets. The script on the 'Roadster' badge remained in black, as it had since the launch of the second generation model.

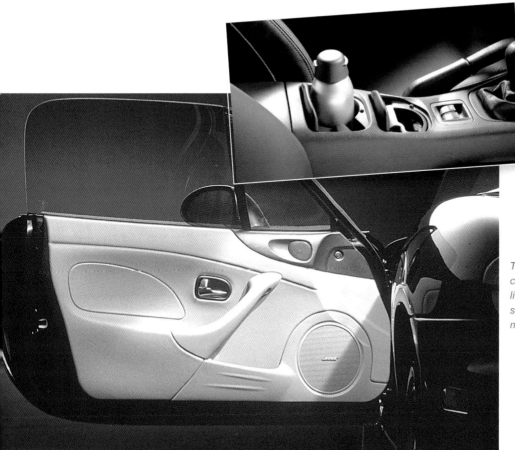

A close-up look at the new cupholder and ashtray arrangement – something the author is happy to do without on a sports car, but considered a necessity in today's market. The cubby aft of the cupholder contained release levers for the bootlid and fuel filler.

The door trim and furniture was also changed as part of the 'NB2' face-lift. This is a home market VS model, so features tan panels instead of the more common black items.

The interior of the VS. All cars now had white gauge faces with red pointers, but again, the needles on six-speed manual models started at the six o'clock position, whilst those on other vehicles started at the eight o'clock position; the calibrations were also different. Note the latest steering wheel design, seen here with a wooden rim (standard on the VS grade). The leather-wrapped wheel looked similar, apart from the obvious difference in materials, although that for the RS-II followed the same two-tone pattern as that established on the 10th Anniversary model.

The author bought this six-speed VS model in Supreme Blue Mica on the first day of sales. Being a VS, it has tan leather trim and a matching hood. It corresponds exactly to original catalogue specifications, and this was its first outing after delivery.

The RS model, designed for better handling performance, features a black interior. The [new] RS-II model features a two-toned interior colour: black and red.

Driving pleasure that gives the feeling of 'Oneness Between Car And Driver'

The Roadster delivers driving pleasure that gives the feel of Oneness Between Car And Driver, which is known as Mazda's 'Dynamic DNA', a development theme common among Mazda's products. The Roadster conveys precise steering and handling, responsive and linear braking, composed and confident ride, and linear and lively performance.

The new Roadster also incorporates improvements to its engine, body and suspension and, as the symbol of the Mazda brand, delivers further improved driving pleasure.

Improved engine performance

The 1.8-litre engine now incorporates the S-VT mechanism that optimizes the open/close timing of the intake valves from low to high rpm ranges. Additionally, the improved intake/exhaust system provides smoother accelerating

An interesting catalogue shot that perfectly illustrates the sculptured curves of the MX-5. The light blue shade (Crystal Blue Metallic) used in most of the publicity material for the new model won the Japan Fashion Colour Association's '2001 Auto Colour Award'.

Japanese advertising for the face-lifted Roadster, dating from the time of launch.

Section of the Japanese brochure devoted to the RS and the new RS-II grade, with its striking interior. Note the Bilstein dampers, additional body reinforcements, the 16-inch wheels and tyres, and the uprated braking system. The car on the right is an RS, as the RS-II was not available in either of the blue shades on offer.

Pages from the Japanese catalogue covering the 1.6-litre models and the 1800S.

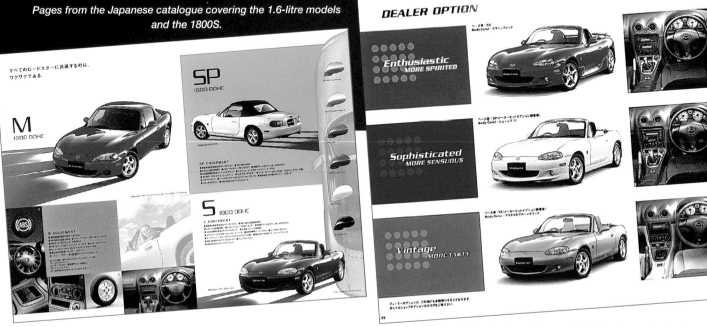

Some of the dealer options available in Japan during the 2000/2001 season.

Advertising for the YS Limited, launched in Japan during December 2000. Only 700 were made available, although there were three exterior body colour choices. This car is finished in Black Mica, a shade unique to this model.

The new model as it appeared in Europe. This is actually a German registered car with the latest 16-inch wheels and tyres.

Tail of the same vehicle. Note the new rear combination light design. Lighting was quite different for the main markets (America, Europe and Japan): US cars had no rear foglight, so the inner sections on the combination lamp were clear on both sides, like those for the home market. All had orange front side markers, but the rears were red on American- and Japanese-spec vehicles, and orange on cars destined for Europe. Another difference concerned the side repeater lights (situated between the front wheelarch and the door), which were not fitted on US cars, but standard on European and Japanese models.

performance up to the high rpm range and attains a sporty and pleasant engine sound. [Maximum power has been increased to 160bhp at 7000rpm.]

More rigid body, improved suspension & newly-adopted tyres
Components that contribute to body rigidity, such as the body frame and crossmembers, have undergone painstaking improvements. The more rigid body results in more solid handling, a smoother ride, and an overall higher quality driving experience.

The RS and RS-II models, which were designed with an emphasis on power and acceleration, are now equipped with 205/45 R16 tyres and lightweight 16-inch aluminium wheels with flat flanges. The body of the RS and RS-II models incorporates reinforcements such as newly-added truss members for substantially increased rigidity.

The RS and RS-II models are equipped with a new type of damper manufactured by Bilstein that has additional valves for controlling the rebound side only. This is the first time these dampers, which contribute to improved driving dynamics, have been offered in Japan.

Enhanced brakes
Enlarged brake components provide improved braking performance with a more responsive feel. Models equipped with 16-inch tyres have larger brake discs, and

Another view of the German car, this time with hood erected. The styling changes, especially when combined with the bigger wheels and tyres, gave the MX-5 a far more aggressive look.

Interior and dashboard of the European MX-5 in left-hand drive guise. The white gauge faces and revised steering wheel (with the Mazda corporate symbol in the centre, and the Nardi badge moving from that position to the lower part of the wheel) can be clearly seen in these pictures.

the brakes on models equipped with 14- or 15-inch tyres have oversized master cylinders and boosters.

For more precise braking, a four-wheel, ABS-enhanced, electronically-controlled braking force distribution (EBD) system, which automatically optimizes the distribution of braking force to match the front and rear load when the brakes are applied, is now available either standard or optional, depending on the model.

Improved seat structure
The seats have been enhanced to provide better support for the shoulder, lumbar, and side areas. This provides drivers with driving pleasure that gives the feel of oneness between car and driver.

More convenience in day-to-day driving
To ensure that the new sports car is enjoyable to drive on a daily basis, the Roadster (continued on page 94)

Cover from the US brochure for the 2001 model year Mazda range. Note the white faces on the instruments, which were soon joined by some red faces in the camp – a blunder in the specifications (namely an engine with "155bhp") was to cause some embarrassment.

Press photograph of the 2001 Miata.

Engine bay of the American Miata LS grade, photographed by Ken Hoyle at the 2000 San Francisco Show, held in November that year. Note the new strut brace design, the same as that used on the home market's RS models.

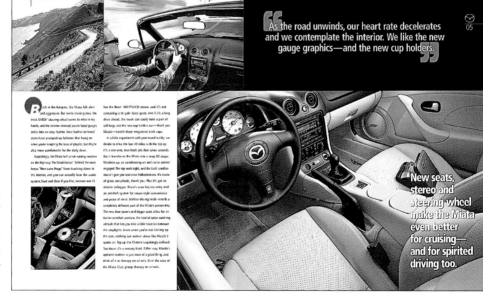

Two double-page spreads from a US brochure put together to advertise the 2001 model year Miata. Note the chrome door handles on the LS grade – a feature added for the 2001 season.

The Miata is the only car ever named an Automobile Magazine All-Star 11 times.

The 2001 model year Miata LS.

The MX-5 has continued to entertain race-goers all over the world. This Miata was being used as a Safety Car during a summer 2001 meeting at Sears Point in California. (Courtesy Ken Hoyle)

A contemporary VS model pictured in Yokohama. In the background, checking out the menu, is Takaharu 'Koby' Kobayakawa, a legendary Mazda figure and the gentleman that signed off the NB1 styling.

features an innovative, upgradeable audio system and a redesigned centre console.

The audio system contains separable audio components. This makes it easy to add more functions in the future, such as a CD changer or an MD player. This audio system configuration shows a new concept that the user can add to the audio system new components including the advanced audio appliance that supports the digital music distribution systems. This Mazda-original audio system provides a new level of post-purchase extensibility.

The size of the centre console box has been increased to accommodate up to six CDs.

The shape and location of the cupholders and ashtray have been modified to make them easier to use. It is also possible to remove the ashtray and use the resulting space as a storage compartment for small objects or another cupholder.

A keyless entry system, including a trunk-lid opener, is available as standard or as an option on certain models. This makes the trunk, which is large enough to accommodate two golf bags, even more convenient.

Enhanced safety

Standard equipment on all models now includes seatbelts with pretensioners and load limiters, as well as the previously offered Supplemental Restraint System (SRS) airbags on the driver and passenger sides.

A few things deserve further explanation, such as the changes to the 1.8-litre twin-cam engine and the body structure, wheel types and sizes (plus the tyres fitted to them), uprated braking systems, and the new gauges.

The 1.8-litre power unit – given the BP-VE (RS) code – received a number of modifications, including adoption of S-VT (Sequential Valve Timing), a hike in the compression

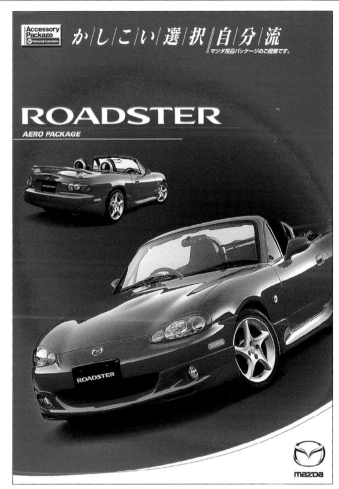

Brochure showing the Aero Package offered by Japanese dealers for the 2001 season. Television commercials from the time showed a plastic model kit box with a standard Roadster on the lid, which opened to reveal movie footage of a real vehicle being driven by an attractive young lady.

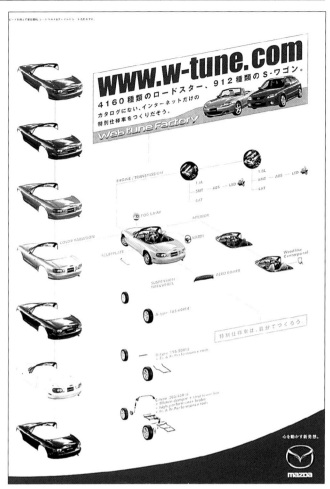

Another piece of Japanese advertising, this time for the so-called Web-Tuned Factory. This enabled buyers to custom order a Roadster or Familia S-WAGON via the Internet; they could even order the open car in the highly desirable Sunburst Yellow, a shade usually reserved for limited editions.

ratio (via new pistons), and subtle refinements in the ignition, intake and exhaust systems. For the home market, power increased to 160bhp at 7000rpm, with maximum torque quoted as 125lbft at 5500rpm.

Buyers in most countries could now specify a six-speed gearbox with the 1.8-litre car. Ratios in Japan were carried over on all transmissions, as were those for the five-speed models destined for US and European markets. Six-speed cars inherited Japan's internal ratios, but the 3.91:1 final-drive was only used in America – European specifications listed a 3.64:1 ratio.

Incidentally, all markets had the same cogs in the automatic transmission (2.450 on first, 1.450 on second, a direct third, and 0.730 on top), with a 4.10 final-drive on the 1.8, or 4.30 on 1.6-litre vehicles.

The body was significantly stronger than before. To quote a different press release: "Additional reinforcements have been made to the body throughout the vehicle. The front and rear inner side sills have a larger cross-section and are made from a thicker plate, the rear floor frame is thicker, and the tunnel gussets have been changed from a short-skirt to a deep-skirt type. These enhancements improved bending rigidity by 13 per cent and torsional rigidity by 6 per cent compared to the 10th Anniversary version, which was the top performance model in the series.

"Exclusive body reinforcements have been added for the 1.8-litre Sport model [the UK equivalent to Japan's RS grade]. The new front suspension tower bar has been reinforced at the head of the suspension tower, the tower bar strengthened, and a tower bar mount adopted. In addition, corner gussets have been added to the rear bulkhead, as well as a trans-member under the floor and a tunnel member behind it, and two rear cross bars added to the rear

The Roadster section from the 2001 Auto Exe tuning catalogue.

The options available on the Web-Tuned Roadster in more detail.

performance bar. Through these improvements, bending rigidity is 16 per cent greater than the 10th Anniversary version, while torsional rigidity is improved by 22 per cent."

Satoru Akana was in charge of the latest styling updates, introduced purely to freshen up the car's appearance in a bid to revive falling sales in Japan, and to make it more appealing to male buyers. Knowing of his love for the original MX-5, the author asked Tom Matano what

he thought of the design. He replied: "The lines have simply got more muscular as engine power has increased. It's a perfect piece of evolution."

Regarding the wheels, steel rims were now something of a rarity, but some markets still received them on the cheapest grade. With a 5.5J width, they came fitted with 185/60 HR14 rubber; the 14-inch five-spoke alloys (6J rim width) were shod with the same tyres.

The cover (right) and a double-page spread from the UK catalogue of May 2001. The car featured in the action photography is a 1.8i Sport model, which had the strut tower bar shown in the ghosted drawing. As European specifications were firmed up, it was noted that all models now came fitted with ABS brakes (incorporating the EBD system) as standard, although there was no change in vehicle pricing.

May 2001 saw the introduction of the limited edition Mazdaspeed Roadster. Only 200 units were made available.

The Mazdaspeed MPS Roadster at the 2001 Tokyo Auto Salon. The 200bhp car was developed under Mazda stalwart, Hirotaka Tachibana, and featured a number of interesting modifications, such as aluminium brake discs, adjustable suspension, and a central exhaust.

The 15-inch alloys were also carried over (6J x 15, with a similar five-spoke design to the 14-inch items), and these came with 195/50-section VR-rated tyres. A new five-spoke alloy wheel with a sharper appearance was introduced to give a 6.5J x 16 option, and this rim was fitted with 205/45 WR16 tyres.

As for the brakes, cars fitted with 16-inch wheels and tyres inherited a larger set of discs – 270mm (10.6in) up front, with 276mm (10.9in) diameter items at the rear. However, the discs continued to be ventilated at the front only, and, whilst ABS was standard in some markets, it was an option in others.

Moving inside the car, perhaps the biggest change was the adoption of white-faced gauges in the meter panel, complete with chrome trim rings around the speedo and tachometer. Mazdaspeed had offered these for some time, and they were a key feature on the NR Limited (and its numerous offspring offered in export markets). White in the daytime with black calibrations, at night they appeared black with amber and red markings – attractive, but, more importantly, very effective in service.

Other less obvious interior modifications included a new storage arrangement in the transmission tunnel area,

The special interior of the MPS model.

Two views of the MPS version of the Roadster unveiled to the public in autumn 2001. It is hoped that this stunning, high performance model can be seen in Mazda showrooms in the very near future.

modified door trim panels, a revised steering wheel design (for both three- and four-spoke items), and new seats incorporating a taller, integral headrest.

The home market

Following the latest revisions to the vehicle, the grades were reshuffled. The 1.6-litre engine still developed 125bhp at 6500rpm, along with 105lbft of torque at 5000rpm. It was available with either a five-speed manual or four-speed automatic gearbox (the latter coming with ABS brakes as standard), but with the basic model gone, the M became the entry-level Roadster.

Priced at 1,839,000 yen (or 1,982,000 yen in automatic guise), the 1600M had power-assisted steering, 14-inch alloy wheels, air conditioning, power door mirrors and windows, and an electric aerial included in the price. The SP was the only other 1.6-litre car, and that came in at 1,990,000 or 2,040,000 yen for the five-speed manual and the automatic respectively. The extra money gave the buyer a Torsen limited-slip differential (manual vehicles only), ABS brakes, a Nardi steering wheel, the Windblocker, and remote control central locking.

The 1.8-litre range was more extensive. The 1800S was roughly the same as the 1600SP, although ABS brakes were standard on the automatic model only. The Windblocker and remote locking became optional,

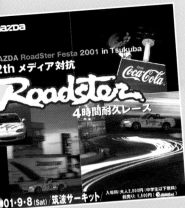

Advertising for the Tsukuba 4-hour Endurance Race – an annual event for Roadster enthusiasts. It is hoped to introduce the race to American shores in the future.

The NR-A pictured at Tokyo Disneyland, the venue for the press preview of Mazda's Tokyo Show exhibits. At this event an official announcement was made that the rotary engined RX-8 would go into production.

At the 2002 Tokyo Auto Salon the Mazda organisation pulled out all the stops. This special brochure, produced by Car Top, gives a good idea of the key exhibits on the company stand. From the top: the Mazdaspeed version of the new Atenza, the RX-7 R-Spec (winner of the 2001-2002 RJC 'Special Award'), Roadster NR-A, Mazdaspeed Roadster MPS, the Cosmo 21 and the RS Coupé.

The UK's equivalent to the MV Limited was the Phoenix MX-5 SE, announced on 14 March 2002, and limited to 1200 units. An Australian version, known as the Titanium MX-5, was released at the same time, priced at $46,595, and limited to just 150 examples.

Cover of the brochure for the 2001 MV Limited.

Exterior and interior views of the US Miata for the 2002 season. An automatic speed-sensing volume control was added to the Bose stereo for 2002, with a six-disc CD available as an option.

although additional features included a leather-wrapped gearknob, and an AM/FM stereo radio with two speakers.

The RS had 16-inch wheels and tyres, a limited-slip differential, uprated suspension with front strut bar and Bilstein dampers, a Nardi leather steering wheel and gearknob, stainless treadplates, an AM/FM radio and rear mudguards, while the RS-II came with a similar specification but red cloth seats, and the Nardi wheel had a two-tone finish. In addition, the remote control locking, Bose sound system and Windblocker were standard.

The VS was the 'luxury' model, with 14-inch five-spoke alloys, a Torsen lsd, tan leather trim with matching hood and hood cover, a Nardi wood-rimmed steering wheel, a wooden gearknob and handbrake grip, the Windblocker, stainless scuff plates, power door locks with remote control (plus chromed interior release handles), and the Bose radio/CD player.

As for prices, the six-speed S was listed at 2,178,000 yen (or 2,226,000 yen with the four-speed ECT), while the manual only RS was 2,328,000 yen; the new RS-II, with its

striking red and black interior (also available with the six-speed gearbox only) was priced at 2,437,000 yen, and the leather-trimmed VS was 2,390,000 yen, and 48,000 yen more if specified with automatic transmission.

Paintwork choices included Crystal Blue Metallic, Sunlight Silver Metallic, Classic Red, Supreme Blue Mica, Pure White and Brilliant Black. The RS-II was not available in the two blue shades, and the VS had to do without the red and silver options, but gained a unique Grace Green Mica colour.

The YS Limited (the YS standing for Youthful & Sports) was officially announced on the 22 December 2000, although RCOJ members were given a sneak preview at the club's Christmas party. Based on the 1600M, it was aimed at younger buyers, mainly because of attractive pricing, but also due to its distinctive interior.

While the body could be finished in Black Mica (a special paintwork colour, only available on the YS Limited), Pure White or Sunlight Silver Metallic, the interior was finished in black with a number of titanium accents. A two-tone black and titanium finish was adopted on the Nardi steering wheel and gearknob, the centre console panel and

door trim featured titanium-style inserts, and there was even titanium coloured stitching on the seats to help give the interior a unique appearance.

Other items included blackout headlamps (the bezel portion of the headlights was black-coated), stainless treadplates, and remote control central locking. Only 700 were made available, priced at 1,797,000 yen for the basic five-speed model (1,828,000 yen with a radio), or 1,940,000 yen for the automatic version.

The new model in Europe

The changes announced in Japan during the summer of 2000 were eventually introduced in European markets the following spring. All of the exterior and interior enhancements were adopted, along with the structural and mechanical improvements. The six-speed gearbox was now part of the standard specification (at least on the 1.8i Sport model), and an automatic transmission – available from August 2001 – was also listed in a bid to try and extend the car's appeal.

With a 10.0:1 compression ratio, the 1.8-litre engine produced 146bhp at 7000rpm in European trim, along

The Arizona – a limited edition MX-5 for the British market, dating from the summer of 2002.

The 333-off Trilogy, made in association with DeBeers, and launched at the end of 2002 alongside the all-weather Montana.

with 124lbft of torque. This was enough to endow the vehicle with a 0-60 time of around 8.5 seconds, and a top speed approaching 130mph (208kph) – the five- and six-speed models were very similar. Automatic versions came with 139bhp at 6500rpm, incidentally, which combined to give an 11 second 0-60 increment, and a maximum of 119mph (190kph).

The 1.6-litre power unit had a 9.4:1 c/r, giving 110bhp at 6500rpm, and 99lbft of torque. Linked to a five-speed gearbox (an automatic transmission was not available with the smaller engine), the official 0-60 figure was 9.7 seconds, whilst top speed was almost identical to that of the automatic 1.8-litre car.

In Britain, Europe's largest market, four grades were available: the 1.6i, priced at £14,995 on the road, the 1.8i (£15,995), the 1.8i Auto (at £16,995) and the 1.8i Sport, which had a sticker price of £17,995.

The basic 1.6-litre model (which weighed in at 1035kg, or 2277lb) had steel wheels shod with 185/60

HR14 tyres, engine speed-sensing power steering, cloth trim, power windows, a stereo radio/cassette with two speakers, dual airbags, remote fuel door and bootlid releases, and an alarm/immobilizer.

The manual 1.8-litre car weighed 30kg (66lb) more in its cheapest form, but only the heavier engine and a Windblocker accounted for the difference. The 1.8i Auto had the same basic specification as the five-speed model, although the automatic transmission added a further 15kg (33lb) to the vehicle's kerb weight.

The six-speed 1.8i Sport added 16-inch alloy wheels shod with 205/45 rubber, ABS brakes (with the larger diameter discs), a limited-slip differential, front foglights (those at the rear were standard on all cars to comply with the law), black leather trim (including on the Nardi steering wheel and gearknob), seat warmers, remote control central locking, chromed inner door handles, stainless treadplates, electrically-adjusted and heated door mirrors, a modular radio/CD unit with four speakers

and an electric aerial, and rear mudguards. The uprated RS-type suspension was available as an option on this 1100kg (2420lb) model, as was a cassette player.

Coachwork colours for Europe included Brilliant Black, Racing Green Mica, Supreme Blue Mica, Eternal Red, Crystal Blue Metallic and Sunlight Silver Metallic, incidentally. Trim was either available in black cloth, or black leather.

News fom the Antipodes

Sales in Australia were at last picking up. After a disastrous 1997 season, in which only 118 MX-5s were imported, 1586 examples made the journey from Japan in 1998. In 1999, this figure dropped to 1263, and again to 1106 in 2000, but it was a very different story to that of three years earlier.

For 2001, the Australians had two basic models to choose from – one with a hard-top and one without. They did, however, get a very high specification vehicle

as standard. Powered by the latest 155bhp version of the 1.8-litre engine, it came with a six-speed gearbox (final-drive ratio 3.64:1), 6.5J x 16 five-spoke alloys shod with wide 205/45 rubber, power-assisted steering, ABS brakes, Bilstein dampers, a front tower bar, foglights, the elegant Nardi leather-wrapped steering wheel and matching gearknob, power windows and door mirrors, remote control central locking, a four-speaker radio/CD player, the Windblocker device, and an engine immobilizer.

Writing for *Wheels* magazine, Peter McKay noticed a tendency for the suspension to bottom out, and also stated: "In any case, the ride is not pleasant as it judders and bangs and leaps over the bumps." However, in most other areas, he was quite complementary about the car, and, after comparing it with the MR2 Spyder, observed: "Chasing the rival MX-5 broader demographic, Toyota has expressed higher volume aspirations for the MR2 Spyder (with younger buyers and more females), built on reduced price and easy-to-drive sequential shift.

Cover of the 2003 model year range brochure for the US, along with the two inner pages devoted to the Miata.

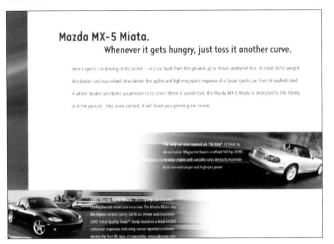

"But it won't grab those people seeking an affordable, traditional sports car. The MX-5 has that parcel tidily wrapped up. The Mazda's classical looks, cult status and excellent retained values – along with its acclaimed dynamics – give it the nod.

"The MR2 Spyder is better than the MX-5 in some ways, but lacks the lineage - and the right gearbox – to make it a winner here. Then again, I'm not a PlayStation regular or Gen Xer ..."

Launched with a tag of $41,190, by summer 2001, the standard six-speed model was priced at $43,485, with the hard-top version coming in at $3000 more. Although the hard-top could be bought separately, there was only actually one real option – air conditioning, priced at $1950. In addition, for those not happy with the factory engine, Mazda Australia's motorsport section prepared a Turbo 'SP' version which developed a healthy 190bhp.

The SP was refined on the 2001 Targa Tasmania before going on sale, and doubtless played a large part in the decision made by head office in Japan to market a turbocharged production version of the Roadster a couple of years down the line.

Wheels magazine tested the $55,540 SP against the Honda S2000 in early 2002. At $11,185 more than the basic model, was the turbocharged MX-5 worth the extra? Apparently so: "In looks, the S2000 has the greater presence, no risk. But the chassis says the engineers need to spend more time going hard behind the wheel and maybe less time on PlayStation. Aside from the terrific engine and awesome gearshift, the S2000 is in some ways unexpectedly ordinary. The SP engine, on the other hand, brings the MX-5 alive, exploiting superior dynamics to the hilt and making this

Cover of the domestic catalogue dating from July 2002, along with the pages for the upgraded VS model.

A regular UK MX-5 from the 2002 season, this model being the 1.8i Sport. Sales in the British Isles were at an all-time high for the Japanese maker.

The Montana special edition, available in either Garnet Red or Racing Green (250 were made of each).

Japanese advertising for the SG Limited of December 2002 vintage.

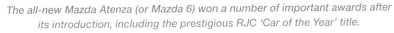

The all-new Mazda Atenza (or Mazda 6) won a number of important awards after its introduction, including the prestigious RJC 'Car of the Year' title.

Launched in 2003, the RX-8 kept the hopes of rotary engine (RE) fans alive, at least for a few years.

Some of the 48 Miatas that took part in the Spec Miata Challenge race at Mazda Raceway Laguna Seca in June 2003.
[Courtesy Ken Hoyle]

Another competitor at Laguna Seca. At grassroots level, the Mazda marque dominates the American racing scene, with Miatas everywhere, and the rotary-powered Star Mazda series providing affordable single-seater action. [Courtesy Ken Hoyle]

hugely driveable package more than a bit extraordinary."

Standard colours for Australia included Classic Red, Grace Green, Supreme Blue (a dark shade), Sunlight Silver, Polar White, Brilliant Black, and Crystal Blue Metallic. The hood and cloth interior trim were available in black only.

The US market

For the 2001 model year (announced in September 2000), the American line-up was revised once again to bring it in line with the Japanese market's cars. Apart from the exterior and interior changes, more power was promised (155bhp was quoted in early catalogues and publicity material), and the six-speed gearbox made a welcome appearance as a cost option.

The base model, with black cloth trim, inherited the 15-inch wheels and tyres, Windblocker and floormats from the previous season's LS, but also gained air conditioning, an anti-theft system (with engine immobilizer), and foglights. Surprisingly, however, the price went down to $21,180, meaning it was $65 cheaper than the previous year's car, despite the additional standard equipment.

The LS, now $23,930, had these new features to augment those already found on the top model, plus the new five-spoke 16-inch wheels shod with ultra-low profile 205/45 tyres, remote control locking, a front strut brace, and what used to be the 1AP Appearance Package - no longer listed as an option. Incidentally, all cars with 16-inch rims acquired the uprated braking system described earlier.

The base model could be upgraded via the Convenience Package (given the CV1 code, it came with remote keyless entry system, power door locks, cruise control, and door-mounted tweeter speakers), priced at $795. The Suspension Package came with an uprated suspension with Bilstein shock absorbers, a front tower bar, Torsen lsd, 16-inch wheels and tyres, and larger

A different meeting at Laguna Seca, this Spec Miata race taking place alongside the ALMS event in September 2003. A Pro version of the SCCA Spec Miata class was introduced in 2004.
[Courtesy Ken Hoyle]

The regular 2003 model year MX-5 for the British market, voted as the best driver's car available for under £15,000 by Autocar magazine. It stated: "The original and still the best of the current generation of affordable sportster, Mazda's evergreen tried-and-tested MX-5 recipe of revvy engine and entertaining rear-wheel drive handling makes it an easy winner."

Cover and selected pages from the domestic catalogue released in September 2003 to coincide with the 2004 model year changes.

Probably only the second mass-produced car in history to be rebuilt by the maker and then resold through its dealers, this is one of the Mazdaspeed Roadsters from the 'Refresh Vehicle' programme, on display at the Tokyo Auto Salon. Deliveries to customers started in March 2003.

The RS Coupé A-Type, readily distinguished by its different grille shape compared to the E-Type version also on display at the Auto Salon.

The 500-off MX-5 Angels, launched in the summer of 2003.

The UK's Nevada limited edition, launched in February 2003.

Mazda UK released one more limited edition MX-5 before the 2003 season ended – the 1.8-litre Indiana.

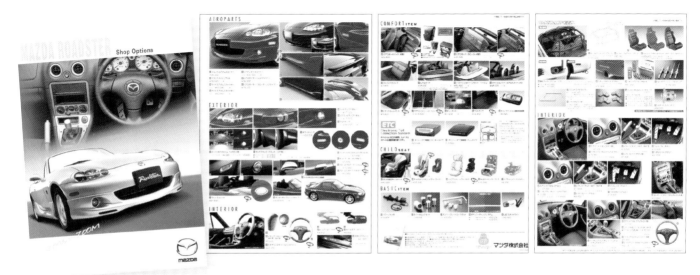

Above: The Japanese accessories brochure for the 2004 season. There was a larger catalogue released at the same time, including greater detail on the parts shown here, audio systems, navigation systems, and other smaller items such as snowchains.

Inner pages from the original Roadster Coupé brochure, showing the four variants available on the home market – the 1.6-litre base model, the 1.8-litre six-speed Type A and Type S, and the 1.8-litre Type E with automatic transmission. The Type A and E could be specified in Lightning Yellow or Velocity Red, while the two cheaper cars came in Pure White, Sunlight Silver or Classic Red.

Of the outside tuners, California's Racing Beat is widely acknowledged as being one of the best – if not the best – in the business. This is the company's Miata parts catalogue from the period.

Miata Style & Sports Line

brakes. Listed at $1025, the suspension pieces were also available on the LS grade for a very reasonable $395.

Interestingly, Patrick Bedard at *Car & Driver* stated: "The Suspension Package, and particularly its grippy tyres, give the Miata a quick-steering, glued-to-the-road feel. Grip matched that of the last test Miata (also 'Packaged') at 0.88g. A good number. But zesty little drop-tops are less about heroic cornering numbers and more about jaunty drifts at recreational speeds. The sticky 16-inch tyres are stingy with their drift angles, even when you blur the scenery. And the Bilsteins hammer over frost-heaved roads. If you're thinking of autocrosses, choose the Suspension Package without hesitation, but for fun and frolic according to the original sports car formula, we strongly prefer the base car."

Other options remained pretty much unchanged, with the obvious exception of those items adopted as part of the standard specification for 2001, although the cassette player was now $150 for all cars (it was previously more expensive on the base vehicle but standard on the LS). There was one interesting addition, though – the option of the six-speed manual gearbox for the LS grade, priced at $650.

Americans had some interesting accessories to choose from: a CD autochanger, front mask, a tonneau cover, treadplates, a wooden dash kit, wooden gearknob, wooden handbrake grip, chrome deck rack, a racing-style fuel filler, front and rear mudguards, a car cover, and even an engine block heater for those living in cold climates.

The colour and trim chart was slightly different to that of the previous season, incidentally, with White being replaced by Pure White, Highlight Silver Metallic being superseded by Sunlight Silver Metallic, and Twilight Blue

Mica giving way to Midnight Blue Mica. By far the biggest change was the loss of Evolution Orange Mica in favour of Crystal Blue Metallic. Trim was still available in either black cloth or tan leather for all of the coachwork hues.

The conclusion at the bottom of the *Car & Driver* test read: "The Miata is better than ever." And most people agreed. As Ann Job of the *San Jose Mercury News* observed: "The new roadster just keeps getting better ... In a slalom, back-to-back test drives of last year's Miata and this year's LS with Suspension Package showed how much more taut and confidence-inspiring this 2001 model is. As you'd expect, I made better time in the new car, too."

At *Motor Trend*, following a comparison test between the standard Miata and an MR2 Spyder, it was noted: "The Miata and MR2 Spyder are the types of cars real enthusiasts spend their weekends driving around in – just because ... The driving sophisticate will get more out of the MR2 Spyder, but the Miata wins in the giggle department."

However, there was an embarrassing moment for Mazda in the States when it was found that the boost in horsepower was nowhere near as large as that advertised – in Japan, yes, but America, no. With a 10.0:1 compression ratio, the power stated in US brochures was quickly revised to 142bhp at 7000rpm, with maximum torque put at 125lbft at 5500rpm.

This makes Patrick Bedard's comments, made at the start of the year, all the more interesting: "Zero to 60 clocked in at 8.1 seconds [with the five-speed car], a half-second behind the old model in the July 2000 issue. A second 2001, with the optional six-speed, hit 60 in 7.9 seconds, still not up to past zip. Both new cars were hampered by green engines and a modest weight increase from reinforcements added to stiffen the body, but it's apparent that 12 or 13 of the promised 15 extra horses weren't answering roll call."

Meanwhile, to avoid possible legal problems, the company contacted its clients and offered to buy back all of the early 2001 models (around 3500 cars) should the owner feel disgruntled after hearing the news. If the owner decided to keep the vehicle, as an apology, they were offered free servicing for the rest of the warranty period. In the end, this potentially damaging mistake was turned into a public relations triumph.

A total of 19,369 Miatas were shipped to the States in 2000, with a further 1349 making their way to Canada.

The present & the future
The Web-Tuned Factory – a way of ordering a custom-built Roadster via the Internet – was launched in February 2001. Customers could access a massive amount

The Ibuki concept car on display at the 2003 Tokyo Show. The word 'ibuki' translates into breath, as in a breath of spring, or a breath of fresh air.

Space age interior of the Ibuki.

The Mazda Roadster Turbo, as portrayed in the brochure handed out at Makuhari Messe.

The revised Web-Tuned Roadster brochure following the changes made to the standard car for the 2004 model year.

A 2004 Miata in its element on the backroads of America ...

of information, delete or add items to get the exact specification they wanted, and even arrange trade-ins and credit in the comfort of their own home. The Web-Tuned Roadster had a total of 4160 combinations to choose from, including Sunburst Yellow coachwork (albeit limited to 450 people) and Sony stereo equipment. For the time being at least, this service was only available for clients living in Japan.

A catalogue issued in spring 2001 confirmed that specifications and colour schemes had been carried over on the standard range. In fact, apart from a new cover picture and an updated line in the keyless central locking specification, it was the same brochure as the one dated July 2000. Prices were carried over, and the 'Shop Options' booklet was also pretty much the same as the original one.

At the 2001 Tokyo Auto Salon, the Mazdaspeed stand featured the 'MPS' Roadster (that particular story is covered later on); a few months later, in May, there was the introduction of another tuned MX-5 – the RS-based limited edition Mazdaspeed Roadster.

Restricted to just 200 units, it featured Starry Blue Mica coachwork, a colour-coded aerodynamic body kit and light trim, gold-painted, 16-inch alloy wheels, a new exhaust system (both to improve efficiency and provide a sporting exhaust note), adjustable dampers (with four settings), uprated engine and differential mounting rubbers, a four-speaker Kenwood stereo, and a number of sporty touches for the interior, such as a carbonfibre-style centre console trim piece, blue coloured gauge trim rings and blue stitching on the seats, steering wheel, gearknob and gearlever gaiter. This special Mazdaspeed vehicle sold for 2,548,000 yen.

After making its debut at the 2001 Chicago Show, the Americans eventually received the Miata Special Edition during the spring. Featuring British Racing Green paintwork, the $26,195 SE (limited to 3000 units) came with the familiar 16-inch alloy wheels but with a polished finish, a tan leather interior with matching hood, a Nardi wood-rimmed steering wheel (a real rarity in the States), wood trim on the six-speed transmission's gearknob and handbrake grip, a wood-look centre console panel, stainless treadplates, a polished aluminium fuel filler cover, and special badging and floormats. Incidentally, by this time, the base model had gone up to $21,660, while the leather-trimmed LS was $24,410.

There was little sign of the MX-5 losing any of its popularity, as Mazda has been very careful not to lose sight of the original LWS concept, whilst still keeping the vehicle contemporary – Kijima-san is adamant that this element, the car's very spirit, will never change.

However, forthcoming noise regulations were of great concern; while the automatic versions will doubtless comply with little problem, something had to be done to quieten the manual cars. Indications point towards the third generation model arriving in 2004, but already, the company was asking RCOJ members for their thoughts on what they would like to see changed and, just as importantly, what they don't want changed. For the record, the author requested the option of a semi-automatic transmission of some sort: I prefer a manual gearbox, but my wife is a two-pedal driver. With a sequential gearbox, we could both enjoy the car ...

The 2001 Tokyo Show
One month before the Tokyo Show, in September 2001, Mazda announced its intentions to run a one-make series in Japan for Roadster owners. Starting in May 2002, it was to be contested over four rounds by 1.6-litre 'NR-A' cars, which could also be registered for road use.

Modifications for the NR-A model included an

Interior of the 2004 Miata, showing the Americans received the same trim changes as the Japanese that season.

A Miata LS on display at the 2004 San Jose Auto Show, held in January that year. Note the new 16-inch wheels, and the optional Appearance Package. [Courtesy Ken Hoyle]

uprated suspension with Bilstein shock absorbers, 15-inch wheels and tyres (6J Enkei five-spoke items, painted white, and shod with 195/50 rubber), larger brakes, increased cooling efficiency (through a larger radiator capacity), reinforced engine and differential mountings, performance rods and other components to stiffen the bodyshell, a limited-slip differential, special seats, and a Nardi steering wheel. For racing, the owner was required to order the Mazdaspeed roll cage, four-point harnesses, and front and rear towing hooks.

The 35th Tokyo Show saw the debut of the production RX-8 and the elegant Atenza saloon, but there was another MPS (Mazda Performance Series) Roadster. The first one had been shown at the Tokyo Auto Salon earlier in the year, and it gave a good idea of what was to come. It was one of two prototypes built to explore the viability of more powerful variants, whilst a third had been produced by Ford in Dearborn, featuring a 210bhp three-litre V6.

This latest MPS car featured a 1.9 litre four (which produced 197bhp at 7000rpm, and 145lbft of torque at 6000rpm) linked to a six-speed manual transmission. The heavily modified body sat on 17-inch wheels and tyres, while the interior featured a black metallic dashboard and a mix of black buckskin and Alcantara fabric for the seating. Sources close to the project stated that, with any luck, the MPS series would reach Mazda showrooms in the spring, but there was still no sign of it at the time of writing.

Meanwhile, the Americans had already announced the 2002 model year changes in September: basically, there was nothing major outlined for the Miata, although the aerodynamic body kit reverted to the options list, with two Appearance Packages (AP1 had a large front airdam, side skirts and rear mudguards, whilst AP2 had smaller skirts and mudguards). Otherwise, all the leading features remained the same, with prices starting at $21,280 (plus delivery charges) for the base model. Coachwork colours included Pure White, Brilliant Black, Classic Red, Midnight Blue Mica, Sunlight Silver Metallic, Emerald Mica, and Crystal Blue Metallic.

In Britain, all cars gained ABS brakes and power door locks for the 2002 season. However, in a bid

A Roadster Coupé being welded. Much of the car was built by hand.

Engine bay of the turbocharged Roadster on Mazda's stand at the 2003 Tokyo Show.

The 700,000th Mazda MX-5 to be built – a turbocharged model for the US, finished in Velocity Red Mica.

Japanese advertising for the Roadster Turbo from the summer of 2004, acknowledging passing the landmark of 700,000 cars built since production started.

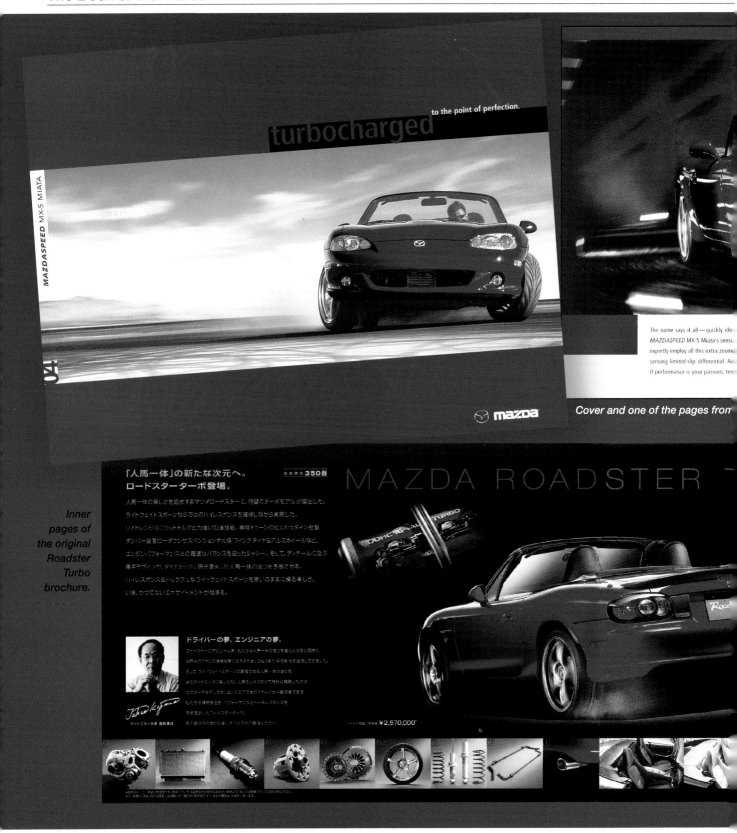

to the point of perfection.

turbocharged

MAZDASPEED MX-5 MIATA

The name says it all—quickly ide
MAZDASPEED MX-5 Miata's sensu
expertly employ all this extra zoom
sensing limited-slip differential. An
If performance is your passion, tes

Cover and one of the pages from

Inner pages of the original Roadster Turbo brochure.

「人馬一体」の新たな次元へ。
ロードスターターボ登場。

全国限定 **350台**

MAZDA ROADSTER

人馬一体の楽しさを追求するマツダロードスターに、待望のターボモデルが誕生した。
ライトウェイトスポーツならではのハイレスポンスを確保しながら実現した、
ワイドレンジのフラットトルクと力強い加速性能。専用チューンのビルシュタイン社製
ダンパー装着ローダウンサスペンションや大径'7インチタイヤ&アルミホイールなど、
エンジンパフォーマンスとの最適なバランスを図ったシャシー。そして、ディテールに及ぶ
専用車デザインが、ダイナミックに研ぎ澄ました人馬一体の走りを予感させる。
ハイレスポンス&トルクフルなライトウェイトスポーツを思いのままに操る楽しさ。
いま、かつてないエキサイトメントが始まる。

ドライバーの夢、エンジニアの夢。

¥2,570,000*

...astest, most potent version of the world's most popular two-seat roadster. Consider it fair warning. For concealed under the ...charged and intercooled 1.8-liter powerplant that churns out a hefty 25% more horsepower. And 33% more torque. To help you ...ed-up, short-throw 6-speed manual gearbox. To translate your choice of gears into meaningful traction, there's a Bosch torque-...andsome hellion with even more tenacious road manners, there's a lowered and sport-tuned double-wishbone suspension. ...*ZDASPEED* MX-5 Miata, before they're all gone, at your *MAZDASPEED* dealer. And soon. Or you may never forgive yourself.

...ated, beautifully-produced six-page Mazdaspeed MX-5 Miata catalogue.

to make the MX-5 more competitive, while the 1.6i remained at £14,995 on the road, the list prices of 1.8-litre cars were reduced by £500. The 1.8i was now £15,495, with the top-of-the-range 1.8i Sport priced at £17,495.

Stop Press

Just before the second edition was finalised, more special cars were launched in Japan. The 1600SP-based MV Limited, announced in December 2001, featured attractive Titanium Grey Metallic paintwork, maroon leather interior (with matching hood cover), new five-spoke, 15-inch alloys, a two-tone Nardi steering wheel, a leather gearknob, aluminium coloured air vents, centre panel and shaft plate, and stainless treadplates; manual cars also came with aluminium pedals. Restricted to just 300 units, it was priced at 2,098,000 yen in five-speed guise, or 2,148,000 yen with automatic transmission.

A sister car was duly launched in the UK during the spring, known as the Phoenix MX-5 SE. Featuring the same Sienna Brown (maroon) seats and Titanium Grey paintwork

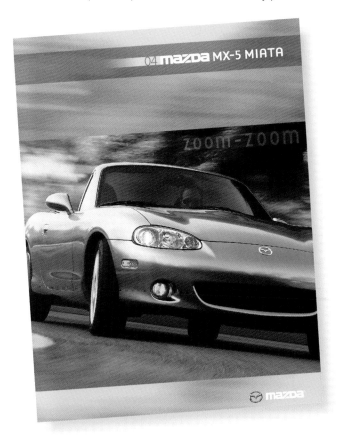

Cover of the 2004 Miata catalogue, featuring new, crisper 'Zoom-Zoom' graphics that would eventually spread to other countries, including Japan.

(although Black was also available in Britain), 15-inch alloys and interior modifications, it was limited to 1200 units and priced at £15,995 in 1.6-litre guise, or £16,595 for the 1.8 (the metallic paint was classed as a £150 option).

Mazda had a massive stand at the 2002 Tokyo Auto Salon, which saw the debut of several important concept vehicles, including a Roadster-based (though rotary powered) Cosmo replica, the RS Coupé, and a silver Roadster MPS with Mazdaspeed badging. The Cosmo 21 and RS Coupé were developed by Mazda's so-called M'zIF subsidiary (under the watchful eye of Shigenori Fukuda), and built by Mazda Sangyo. The RS Coupé is, perhaps, the most interesting of the two, as it stands more chance of being seen in the showrooms. Speaking to the author, Fukuda-san said it was designed to "encompass styling cues from the entire Ford family." The front does hint strongly at the RX-8, the tail is definitely Aston Martin-like, and there are shades of Jaguar in there, too.

The Mazdaspeed Roadster MPS featured an open body, strengthened by a roll-over cage, a substantial front strut bar, and the same underbody bracing as that on the Tokyo Show coupé. With a 185bhp version of the 1.8-litre four linked to a six-speed gearbox, it had the performance to back up its aggressive looks; a sporty, purposeful interior, deep airdam, separate headlights, flared wheelarches, various cut-outs in the panels, a rear spoiler, 7J x 17 OZ alloys shod with 215/40 rubber, and twin exhaust pipes (a Tachibana trademark) exiting from the centre of the rear valance. Mention should be made of the beautifully prepared engine bay, with its carbonfibre-type air filter housing and radiator garnish, a black crackle finish on the cam cover, and polished exhausts – a true piece of automotive sculpture. Maximum power was produced at 7000rpm, incidentally, with 133lbft of peak torque coming in at 6000rpm.

In keeping with Mazda's sporting image, the 'Zoom-Zoom' advertising campaign started in Japan in spring 2002, becoming a global message as the months passed. If you get the chance, read all the text on the full motor show version – for sports car fans it certainly strikes a chord, as it describes the love of motion that we felt in childhood and simply never lost.

Mazda gained a new President in April 2002 in the shape of Lewis Booth. The amiable Booth was a definite sports car guy, driving an RX-7 during his time in Japan, but an appointment with Ford in Europe was calling, and his stay was to be a short one.

Time was also running out for the RX-7, the last one rolling off the line in August 2002. This left Mazda without a rotary-engined model until the official launch of the RX-8 in April 2003, although a new line of conventional engines – the MZR series – had made its debut by mid-2002, these lightweight, all-alloy twin-cam units finding service in the Atenza saloon and the MPV. The MZR would become an important part of the MX-5 story in due course.

Stateside update

Japan was not the only country to be treated to a new MX-5 race series, America had the Mazdaspeed Cup for 2002, the first round taking place at Laguna Seca, where no less than 70 Miatas took to the grid.

In the meantime, the Chicago Show witnessed the debut of two SE models for 2002 – one in Titanium Grey, and a second version in Blazing Yellow. The grey car was trimmed in saddle brown leather, while the yellow model was treated to a black leather interior, complete with a Miata logo embroidered into the seatback. Both six-speed cars had 16-inch Enkei alloy wheels, a chrome fuel filler, an in-dash 6-CD autochanger to go with the Bose stereo, white-faced gauges with aluminium accent rings, a Nardi leather steering wheel, gearknob and handbrake covering, aluminium door handles, aluminium pedals, aluminium scuff plates, and special badging. A Torsen lsd, ABS brakes, foglights and a body kit could be specified as options.

Press invitation to see the SE Miatas at the 2002 Chicago Show.

American Miata sales were slowing down. and a total of 15,622 cars were sent across the Pacific in 2002 compared to 17,575 in the previous year. Still, given the increased competition in the open sports car market and the fact that the little Mazda had barely changed visually since 1997, the figures were perfectly acceptable.

A minor change for Japan

The Roadster was treated to what the Japanese term a 'minor change' (or MC) in July 2002. All cars benefited from an ISO-FIX child seat anchor on the passenger side, and revised A-pillar trim to reduce head injury in the event of an accident. Water-repellant door and mirror glass became standard across most of the range (the M and NR-A grades had to do without). The Bose sound system could now be specified on 1.6-litre cars as an option, and stainless treadplates were now fitted on all automatic models.

A Blazing Yellow SE on display in the Windy City.

The top-of-the-range VS grade was now split into two separate variants – the sporty VS Combination A, and the classic VS Combination B. The Combination A came with black leather upholstery, a black cloth hood (replacing the traditional vinyl one), all-black trim, and aluminium accents on the centre console and air vent bezels. The Combination B had a beige interior (like that of the old VS, but a slightly different shade to that previously employed), a beige fabric hood, and darker wood trim than before to give the car an elegant look.

The paintwork colour chart was altered at the same time, with Crystal Blue giving way to two new shades – Splash Green Mica, and Garnet Red Mica. The six remaining hues in the line-up were carried over, matched up with either black leather or cloth, beige leather, or red cloth depending on the grade and coachwork colour.

The production changes took place in early July, while the fresh colours and new VS grades were due to reach showrooms in the following month. Prices ranged from 1,839,000 yen for the 1.6-litre manual M, up to 2,446,000 yen for the latest automatic VS models, although there were plenty of options to tempt Japanese buyers. The contemporary Shop Options catalogue ran to 18 pages, broken down into Mazdaspeed accessories, and parts that were aimed at those striving for an 'Enthusiastic,' 'Vintage' or 'Sophisticated' look.

The UK story continues

After the Phoenix, the next special edition launched in the UK was the Arizona. The Arizona, announced on 28 June 2002, was available in three colours (Sunlight Silver, Blaze Yellow or Eternal Red) and was powered by either a 1.6 or 1.8-litre engine. The £16,095 1.6-litre car gained unique 15-inch alloys, black leather seat trim with silver stitching, seat heaters and style bars (roll-over hoops), a windblocker, stainless scuff plates, aluminium console and dash trim, remote central locking (with boot release), a black leather Nardi wheel with silver stitching (plus matching gearknob and handbrake trim), power mirrors, a CD player, and an electric aerial. The £16,695 1.8-litre model also came with a Torsen limited-slip differential; mica or metallic paint was classed as a £250 extra.

For the 2003 model year, although prices were carried over on the 1.6i and 1.8i models, all British cars gained heated power mirrors, an electric aerial, a low fuel warning light, and an ISO-FIX child seat anchor; a factory-fitted satellite navigation system was listed as a £1500 option. At the same time, the 1.8i Sport was given a fabric hood (optional on lesser grades, combined with 15-inch alloys), chrome fuel filler lid and Bilstein dampers, adding £500 to the sticker price, which now stood at £17,995.

Two more limited editions for the UK market were launched in the autumn, the 1.8i-based Trilogy, and the Montana. The Trilogy was produced in association with the famous DeBeers concern, being finished in Black with light grey leather trim. Special features included a black cloth top, chrome-plated 15-inch alloys, a two-tone steering wheel and gearknob, unique 'Trilogy' treadplates and badges, chrome fascia accents and inner door handles, a CD player (with extra speakers), and a solid silver keyring set with three diamonds – the signature theme of the Trilogy jewelry line.

The £16,995 Trilogy was joined by the £18,995 Montana, which came in either Garnet Red or Racing Green (250 examples of each colour were available). In addition to the regular 1.8i features, the Montana had a body-coloured hard-top, a fabric hood, 15-inch five-spoke alloys, foglights, air conditioning, heated tan leather seats, a Nardi leather steering wheel and gearknob, a wood-trimmed handbrake, a wood-type centre console, treadplates, chrome inner door handles, tan carpets, an upgraded stereo, and remote central locking.

It was a record year for MX-5 sales in the UK, with over 7000 cars finding new homes during the 2002 calendar year – a big percentage of the 19,663 units sold across the whole of Europe.

America's 2003 season

Mazda North America announced the 2003 models on 16 September 2002 with the following words: "The world's best-selling sports car, the Mazda MX-5 Miata, remains true to the concept of 'oneness between car and driver' with the addition of a special performance package designed for owners who want to race their cars.

"High-performance 205/45 WR16 radial tyres offered previously as upgrade equipment are now standard on all Miatas, with 16-inch aluminium wheels and wheel locks. The proven 1.8-litre, 142bhp four-cylinder engine under the Miatas hood achieves its free-breathing spirit by means of a dohc 16v cylinder head design and a 10.0:1 compression ratio. Variable valve timing on the intake tract pumps the peak power point up to a stirring 7000rpm. The torque curve reaches its crescendo with 125lbft at 5500rpm.

"Special performance package [Club Sport] Miatas, production of which is limited to just 50 units – 25 soft-top and 25 hard-top models – were developed for the hardcore club enthusiast. Starting with a base Miata (with suspension package), the special performance package-equipped models receive further suspension fine-tuning and are lightened by removing the power steering, modular audio system, power antenna and air conditioning.

"Racers who participate in SCCA Solo I, Solo II or ProSolo series should find that the soft-top model with the special performance package fits the bill perfectly, while hard-top models equipped with the package are designed to be competitive in SCCA Showroom Stock racing, once a rollbar and required safety equipment are installed.

"The Miata and Miata LS models come standard with amenities such as a Nardi leather-wrapped steering wheel, front and rear independent double-wishbone suspension, gas-filled shock absorbers, front and rear stabilizer bars, front suspension tower brace, power-assisted four-wheel ventilated disc brakes, power steering, power windows, power mirrors and air conditioning.

"In addition to these standard features, the 2003 Miata LS adds leather seats, cruise control, remote keyless entry system, power door locks, a 200W Bose AM/FM/CD modular audio system with four speakers and automatic speed-sensing volume control. It also adds a new cloth convertible top, aluminium-like interior trim, and two new interior colours – black and parchment.

"With all of Miata's improved designs, the 2003 models are great for any driver looking for a fast, fun and affordable roadster."

The Miata had certainly taken on a more sporting stance, with 16-inch alloys standard across the board, and a front strut tower brace added to the base model to make that another standard feature on all cars. A five-

speed manual gearbox was still the norm, however, with a six-speed adding $650 (available on the LS only), and automatic transmission costing $800.

Options were pretty much the same after the new specifications had been taken into account, with only front and rear light bezels, a cargo net, and a rearview mirror-mounted compass and outside temperature gauge being notable additions.

Coachwork colours now included Classic Red, Splash Green Mica, Sunlight Silver Metallic, Brilliant Black, Pure White, Garnet Red Mica, Midnight Blue Mica, and Emerald Mica; the strict Miata's hood came in black vinyl, while the LS had either a black or parchment cloth one. Interiors were trimmed in either black cloth, or black or parchment leather on the LS grade.

Sticker prices were only slightly up on those for 2002, with the basic Miata costing $21,605, whilst the standard LS commanded $24,385. Incidentally, MNAO had more than 700 dealers across the States at this time.

Once again, Mazda chose the Chicago Show in February to unveil its annual limited edition model, but this year there were two – the $23,105 Shinsen Version, and the $26,030 Special Edition, both restricted to 1500 units apiece.

The Shinsen had Titanium Grey paintwork, a dark blue hood, and dark blue cloth seat trim. Sporting a limited-slip differential, it was also fitted with a Convenience Package (the car was based on the strict Miata), dark blue door inserts, a two-tone leather gearknob, embroidered floormats, and aluminium interior trim pieces.

Based on the six-speed LS, the Special Edition was given unique 16-inch alloys, Strato Blue Mica coachwork, a grey cloth hood, and grey leather trim for the seats. The 2003 SE also had a chrome fuel filler door, aluminium treadplates, aluminium pedals, a leather-wrapped handbrake, and a six-CD autochanger. A certificate was presented with the car, along with a pair of baseball caps, a backpack/cooler, a blanket, and a game set.

American journalist Rexx Taylor said of the Special Edition: "The SE is a real attention getter and a pretty neat sports car. Like all Miatas built since production started over 13 years ago, this is one fun ride."

Mazda's Christmas present

A week before Christmas 2002, Mazda announced the SG Limited for the domestic market. Based on the 1.6-litre NR-A or 1.8-litre RS, the SG Limited featured redesigned 15- and 16-inch five-spoke alloys, Bilstein dampers, uprated brakes with ABS, Cerion Silver Metallic paint, a blue cloth soft-top, blue cloth seats, blue door trim, a blue/black leather steering wheel and gearknob, a leather-wrapped handbrake, aluminium-look interior accent pieces, remote keyless entry, and a

Bose sound system. Only 400 units were made available in all, the five-speed 1600 SG Limited costing 2,150,000 yen, while the six-speed 1800 commanded 300,000 yen more.

As the New Year rolled around, it was once again time for the Tokyo Auto Salon. Traditionally, Auto Salon plays host to a wealth of tuning cars, with the maker stands flooded with new vehicles with various aerodynamic appendages and bolt-on mechanical goodies. Mazda had its fair share of such models, but there was also an old car on the stand – a Mazdaspeed Roadster from the 'Refresh Vehicle' scheme.

Nissan was first to come up with the idea of rebuilding old vehicles and reselling them through dealers, the Datsun 240Z getting the full treatment before the Z33 came along. Now Mazda, through Mazda E&T (Mazda Engineering & Technology Co Ltd), was restoring first generation Roadsters, and selling them on again at prices starting from as low as 1,430,000 yen. 30 cars were scheduled to go through the programme initially, each built to customer specifications.

The RS Coupé from the previous year was popular enough to warrant another outing, with A-Type and E-Type versions on display, the two models featuring subtly different coachwork and interior trim. The RS Coupé eventually found its way into Mazda showrooms, but for the time being, enthusiasts had to be content with dreaming about ownership.

Actually, there was one other RS Coupé – an NR-A version, but only the regular Roadster NR-As were allowed to enter the Party Race one-make series. Four races were planned for 2003, as had been the case in 2002 (the inaugural year), allowing drivers to enjoy flat-out track work at reasonable cost.

Across the State line ...

The last British MX-5 special editions had been named after western states in America. The next one in line, announced on 24 February 2003 and limited to 2050 units, moved further west, adopting the Nevada moniker.

Available with either the 1.6 or 1.8-litre engine, and with a choice of Cerion Silver or Strato Blue paintwork, the Nevada was equipped with unique 16-inch alloys, a dark blue or grey cloth soft-top (with matching hood boot), a two-tone leather steering wheel and gearknob, an aluminium-look centre panel, stainless treadplates, a windblocker, and the option of leather trim on the 1839cc model. The MX-5 Nevada 1.6i was priced at £15,995, with the 1.8-litre engine adding £500 to the invoice; leather upholstery increased the bill by another £500.

Hot on the heels of the film *Charlie's Angels: Full Throttle* came another limited edition – the MX-5 Angels. Announced on 30 July 2003, the Angels featured multi-spoke 15-inch alloys, black leather

The two limited edition Miatas introduced at the 2003 Chicago Show, with the SE in the foreground.

seats with red stitching, a rear spoiler, roll-over hoops, a windblocker, a chrome-type centre console panel, a CD player, and special badging on the treadplates and side of the vehicle. Available in Eternal Red or Sunlight Silver, it was also possible to specify the 1.6 or 1.8-litre engine at the time of ordering.

Six weeks later, just before the 2003 season came to an end, yet another limited edition was launched – the 1.8-litre MX-5 Indiana. This car, limited to 250 units priced at £17,000 apiece, was finished in Garnet Red with a beige leather interior, and came with a wood-rimmed steering wheel and various wooden accents to give the vehicle a classic look.

News from the homeland

In August 2003, Hizakazu Imaki became President and CEO at head office – the first Japanese boss at Mazda in a long time. This immensely likeable character – and a Mazda man through and through – was recently voted RJC 'Person of the Year' in recognition of his firm but caring leadership that has allowed the Hiroshima maker to post record profits for the 2004-2005 fiscal year, despite a crippling fire in December 2004 that shut down the massive Ujina No.1 plant for four months.

Not long after Imaki's appointment, the Roadster received another face-lift in time for the 2004 season. With sales starting on 18 September 2003, the revised models

Tail of the American version of the turbocharged car, this angle showing off its unique badging.

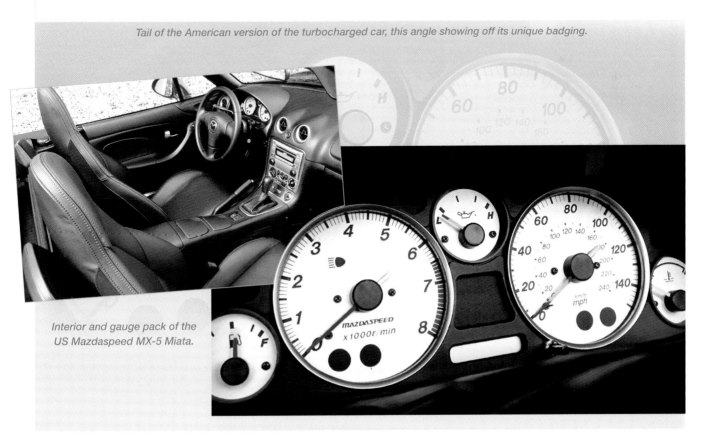

Interior and gauge pack of the US Mazdaspeed MX-5 Miata.

The MX-5 Arctic limited edition from summer 2004, seen here with the optional hard-top in place. A unique package of rear style bar, soundboard, chrome filler cap, and chrome door handles and mirrors was available at a heavily discounted price on this model.

Cockpit of the UK's MX-5 Euphonic special edition. It cost £16,500 for the 1.6i version, and £500 more for the 1.8i-based model.

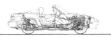

featured a number of exterior and interior enhancements, plus extra standard equipment on a number of grades.

All cars received aluminium-style accent pieces, including the console centre panel, the shift plate, meter and air vent bezels, the inner door handles, and the handbrake release button, aping the VS Combination A trim introduced for the 2003 model year. A vanity mirror on the passenger-side sunvisor was also fitted across the board from this time.

The Bose audio system was upgraded to a 225W unit with six speakers, whilst cars fitted with the windblocker (all grades except the M and NR-A for 2004) gained two tweeters built into the aeroboard, along with a handy mesh cargo net beneath it.

The fitment of water-repellant door and mirror glass was extended to the M grade, and more options were made available for the NR-A, making it a far more practical proposition for everyday use.

Moving up the ladder, a new 6.5J x 16 five-spoke wheel design was adopted for the RS and RS-II, suitably shod with 205/45 rubber. There was also, at last, a leather-covered handbrake lever for these sporty models.

New paintwork options, including Titanium Grey Metallic II, Radiant Ebony Mica and Strato Blue Mica were introduced, respectively replacing Splash Green Mica, Garnet Red Mica and Supreme Blue Mica on the colour chart; interior colour schemes remained unchanged, although cars with cloth trim received a new, improved material.

Prices ranged from 1,850,000 yen for the manual M to 2,455,000 yen for the RS-II. Interestingly, at the time of the face-lift announcement, Mazda joined forces with hip-hop artist Zeebra in its advertising campaign in an attempt to reach out to the youth market that seems determined to buy one-box vehicles rather than sports cars. Anyway, Zeebra also used a customized Roadster in the video promoting his album, entitled *Tokyo's Finest*.

After a protracted birth, the Roadster Coupé was finally brought to market on 9 October 2003, available through Mazda Anfini dealers or customer order direct to the factory. The delay in introducing this elegant model had been caused by keeping costs down to a minimum, allowing prices to start at a reasonable 2,350,000 yen.

Only a few new stampings were required to convert the drophead MX-5 into a Roadster Coupé, limited to the roof, trunk assembly and rear quarters, plus the odd strengthening piece and an inner rear window support to mate up to the large rear wing pressing that included the rear window pillar. Exterior trim, executed in either carbonfibre or glassfibre, then distinguished the Type A and Type E from each other and the more standard-looking Type S and base model.

Actually, at first sight, the two lower grades looked almost identical to their convertible stablemates, unless one could see the car in profile, or from the rear. The Type E had a different front bumper moulding, unique headlight bezels, and rear combination light trim from the Mazda options brochure, while the Type A had another front bumper moulding (with a carbonfibre lip spoiler), side skirts, rear valance trim, a rear spoiler, fender flares, and front and rear light bezels. All parts, except the two sets of light covers (which were sourced from the Shop Options catalogue), were original, unique to the Type A Coupé.

Base vehicles included the 5MT SP for the basic Coupé, the RS for the Type S and Type A, and the 4AT VS Combination B for the Type E. As a matter of interest, the Type A Coupé weighed in at 1100kg (2420lb), the same as the Type S; the Type E tipped the scales at 1090kg (2398lb), while the basic tin-top car was 1040kg (2288lb). For comparison, standard Roadster kerb weights ranged from 1030kg (2266lb) to 1080kg (2376lb) at that time.

The top-of-the-range Type A (priced at 3,100,000 yen) and the 2,800,000 yen Type E would only be sold until the end of April 2004, limited to 200 and 150 units respectively, whereas the base car and Type S were allowed to continue for as long as demand existed. Amazingly, on release, the Roadster Coupé became Japan's only rear-wheel drive Coupé with an engine capacity of under two-litres on the domestic market.

The Ibuki concept car made its debut at the 2003 Tokyo Show – an open two-seater that reminded the author of a little boat. I remember speaking to Kijima-san at Makuhari, and the concern on my face must have been blindingly obvious. "Don't worry, Brian-san," he said, "the new car looks very different!"

The other convertible car on the Mazda stand to make a world premiere was the Roadster Turbo, but more on that particular model later ...

US update

America's 2004 model year changes pretty much reflected those of Japan's, with the revised 16-inch wheel and tyre combination coming online, aluminium-look interior trim being adopted across the board, along with the upgraded windblocker arrangement and vanity mirror. There was also a new colour palette, with Brilliant Black, Pure White, Sunlight Silver Metallic, Emerald Mica and Classic Red being joined by two new shades – Strato Blue Mica and Black Cherry Mica; interior options remained the same.

The ratios on the five-speed manual transmission were carried over (they were still the same as those specified at the time of the second generation Miata's launch), as were those for the automatic transmission. However, the optional six-speed gearbox gained a new final-drive ratio. While it had previously used the Japanese internal ratios and rear axle ratio, for 2004, the US 6MT cars went from a 3.91:1 to a 4.10:1 final-drive, as per the automatics.

With exchange rates quoted as 110 yen to the $1 at the time, prices started at $21,868 for 2004 (only around $200 up on the previous year), with leading options such as a six-speed gearbox ($650), ABS brakes ($550), a detachable hard-top ($1500), and a number of packages there as always to tempt the buyer. The only new option was a set of door edge guards, priced at $45.

Shortly after the 2004 changes were announced, export figures were released from Japan showing another fall in US MX-5 shipments, down to 11,999 units in the 2003 calendar year. Despite roaring sales of the RX-8, Mazda 6 (Atenza) and Mazda 3 (Axela), the figure would fall again in 2004, to 10,502 cars, but Mazda already had an answer on how to boost sales waiting in the wings ...

In the meantime, the 700,000th MX-5 was built on 5 March 2004. It happened to be an American-spec Mazdaspeed MX-5 Miata that went on sale in the States that month, which was actually the same car as the Roadster Turbo for the home market.

Having made its debut at the Tokyo Show, the Roadster Turbo eventually went on sale in the Land of the Rising Sun in the early part of February 2004. Limited to 350 units in Japan, the main ingredient in the Turbo package was of course the engine – in addition to the IHI

single-scroll blower, which improved low-down torque by up to 20 per cent, there was also an air-to-air intercooler, a large bore exhaust, a larger radiator and oil cooler, Iridium sparkplugs, and a beautiful red camshaft cover. With a 9.5:1 compression ratio (thanks to modified piston crowns) and a relatively low 7psi of boost, the 1839cc BP-ZET (RS) engine delivered 172bhp at 6000rpm, and 154lbft of torque at 5500rpm.

In keeping with the power increase, the clutch and six-speed transmission parts were suitably uprated, along with the engine mounts, the propshaft, torque-sensing limited-slip differential, and the driveshafts. At the same time, the final-drive ratio was dropped to 4.10:1, the suspension was lowered by 7mm/0.27in. and stiffened up (via Bilstein shock absorbers, 20 per cent harder springs and beefier anti-roll bars), the brake calipers were painted silver (ABS and EBD came as standard), the rack was modified to give quicker steering, and Racing Hart 7J x 17 five-spoke alloys were adopted, finished in a silver-grey hue and shod with 205/40 rubber.

The car was given a new front airdam (with foglights), rear spoiler and rear valance skirt, smoked light bezels, and special badging. Inside, the black leather steering wheel was given red stitching (a theme carried over to the gearknob and handbrake); there was a special rearview mirror with the Roadster logo, a Bose stereo with a six-CD

Tail of the 2005 model year Mazdaspeed MX-5 Miata.

autochanger, silver gauges, a patterned centre console, stainless treadplates, and a drilled aluminium pedal set. A black cloth interior with red inserts on the seats and door panels was considered standard, but it was also possible to specify an all-black cloth trim, beige leather upholstery, or black leather with red stitching.

The domestic Turbo weighed in at 1120kg (2464lb), with prices starting at a very reasonable 2,570,000 yen. Coachwork colours included Velocity Red Mica, Pure White, Sunlight Silver Metallic, and Grace Green Mica.

The US Turbo made its official debut at the LA Show, going on sale in the spring of 2004. In keeping with the car's Stateside moniker, the US version was adorned with various Mazdaspeed logos, but was otherwise virtually the same specification as the home market machine, despite slightly different power and torque outputs being quoted.

In America, the $25,500 turbocharged model was available in Velocity Red or Titanium Grey only, with a black vinyl hood, and the black/red cloth interior seen in Japan. For $700 extra, one could specify the Grand Touring Package, which brought with it a black fabric hood and black leather trim.

Car & Driver noted: "The turbo installation is what you'd expect from a big-name factory: tidy and professional, with neat touches like induction resonators to cut obnoxious noise ... The Mazdaspeed car feels wholly transformed, capable of top gear traffic slaloms at just a jab of the throttle. The turbo itself is virtually transparent."

The magazine concluded: "It's a screaming deal because any decent aftermarket turbo kit would cost at least three grand and wouldn't come with Mazda's warranty or the suspension bits."

Autoweek liked the car's build quality and styling, it's handling, power, steering feel, and the Bose stereo. On the down side, it felt the cockpit was a touch tight, as was the trunk, and the clutch was too close to the footrest. It also mourned the loss of the Miata's cruise control, and was surprised to find no boost gauge. Still, 'bang for buck' was what it was all about, and 0-60 in 6.6 seconds and a standing-quarter time of 15.1 seconds was certainly impressive for a car in this class, as was a 0.9g lateral acceleration figure on the skidpan.

The European market for 2004

Britain seemed to be holding up MX-5 sales in the EEC, accounting for a good percentage of the 18,931 cars shipped to Europe in 2003, and the 13,900 sent from Japan in 2004. Indeed, around 9000 MX-5s were sold in the UK during 2003 – almost the same number of cars sold across the entire Continental mainland.

Despite the various improvements inherited from the 2004 model year home market machines (new wheels, windblocker, interior trim, et cetera, as well as the three new paintwork shades), prices were carried over from previous season, ranging from £14,995 to £17,995. For

UK MX-5 sales continued to be strong in the second generation's final year ...

Exterior and interior views of the British MX-5 for the 2004 model year. Note the new 16-inch alloys on the 1.8i Sport, and the latest interior (this example featuring black leather trim).

sake of comparison, the cheapest Mazda was the £8760 Mazda 2, while the RX-8 line started at £20,000. Exchange rates at this time stood at about 200 yen to £1, by the way.

The first limited edition of the season was announced in mid-January 2004, taking interior styling cues from the Roadster Turbo. The 2000-off MX-5 Euphonic, as it was called, featured unique 16-inch alloys, a top Sony stereo system, black and red leather trim (with matching door panels), red stitching on the leather-trimmed steering wheel, gearknob and handbrake, stainless scuff plates, a windblocker, and a black fabric hood. Coachwork colour options included Velocity Red Mica, Titanium Grey Metallic, Brilliant Black, and Sunlight Silver.

Just one more special edition was released during the same season – the MX-5 Arctic of August 2004 vintage. Like the Euphonic, it was based on either the 1.6i or 1.8i, but cost £500 more. For the extra money, 2000 lucky customers got unique, 15-inch multi-spoke alloys, chrome side window garnish, a blue cloth soft-top and boot, air conditioning, heated blue leather seats (with matching door trim), remote central locking, a CD player with six speakers (including the two in the windblocker), chrome treadplates, and black leather on the steering wheel, gearknob and handbrake. As well as the regular Titanium Grey and Sunlight Silver shades, the Arctic model was also available with Razor Blue Metallic paintwork.

Update from Down Under

Historically, sales in Australia were hardly strong, possibly due to the lay of the land and the climate, but the MX-5 certainly had an enthusiastic following. Between January 2001 and December 2004, 2645 Roadsters made the journey south to find new homes Down Under. However, whilst Europe had to live without the turbocharged MX-5, Australian enthusiasts were given the opportunity to buy one in March 2004; while it carried Mazdaspeed badges in America and the Roadster Turbo moniker in Japan, the Aussie's called it the MX-5 SE.

Making its official debut at the Melbourne Show, Mazda Australia's Malcolm Gough said of the turbocharged car: "The addition of the $45,490 SE adds a new and very exciting dimension to the world's best-selling sports car.

"This car represents the biggest change to the MX-5 in years, yet it stays true to the original roadster formula while delivering more of all the great things so many buyers love about the MX-5.

"The SE's enhanced dynamics package, underpinned by a user-friendly torquey engine, will further demonstrate why the MX-5 has earned its icon sports car status. It will offer an unrivalled driving experience and great value."

The new SE was actually significantly cheaper than the Australia-only SP, and leather trim could be specified

for just $1000 more. The SE was available with either Velocity Red, Sunlight Silver or Titanium Grey paintwork.

Wheels tried the car new as soon as it was released, and declared: "There was a whole lot more to developing the SE than just bolting on a snail, winding up the wick, and letting it rip. Bluntly, that was more the preserve of the Australian-developed MX-5 SP. But don't get me wrong – that car's 150kW rendition of petite sports car power was exhilarating, and hardly rough around the edges. It's just that the SE adopts a more softly-softly approach to MX-5 performance enhancement.

"The MX-5 SE has better than adequate performance, accelerating strongly through all six of its manually selected gears (no auto is offered), with just a hint of turbo-lag low in the rev-range to indicate this is a force-fed motor. On full throttle the exhaust can give a pop as boost is off-loaded close to the rev limit, but, for the most part, acceleration is distinctly non-turbo-like, and as linear as the standard car. There's just more of it.

"What's apparent is that the SE isn't so much a hyper version of the existing MX-5 compromised by the quest for speed, but more a natural and incremental progression of its strengths. Perversely, it has taken plenty of engineering to hold things in check, but the main is that, for a scant $45,000, the SE is even more entertaining than the original. And that's saying plenty."

The regular Australian six-speed MX-5 was priced at $40,530 for the 2004 season, with automatic transmission adding $1500. Prices and specifications on all MX-5 variants were carried over for 2005.

Bowing out gracefully

There were no changes posted in Japan for the 2005 model year. Indeed, apart from an odd minor graphics change (like the 'Zoom-Zoom' insignia) and a single page rearranged to include a small section on the Roadster Coupé, the same catalogue issued a year earlier was reprinted. The same was basically true of the Roadster Turbo brochure, although the dark green paint scheme had disappeared by the time the 2005 season started.

In the States, also, there was nothing much to report – a retractable key on the remote central locking hardly counts as a major change, even if it was a run-out year. There were a couple of colour schemes added, however, including Razor Blue and Nordic Green, augmenting Black Cherry, Classic Red and Sunlight Silver on normally-aspirated cars. The Mazdaspeed model was available in two new shades (namely Black Mica and Lava Orange Mica), plus Titanium Grey and Velocity Red carried over from 2004; silver stitching became available alongside the existing red for the leatherwork. Prices started at $22,098 for the base model and went up to $25,780 for the turbocharged car.

Various views of the 2005 1.6-litre SP bought by the author's wife – one of the last Second Generation Roadsters built. Note the automatic gearbox, and the registration number paying homage to Mazda's Le Mans win in 1991 (also used on the family RX-8 at the time, and any other new Mazdas joining the household after that).

The MX-5 Icon was the last special edition based on the NB2 (seen here finished in Chilli Orange Mica). Available from April 2005, the Third Generation MX-5 had already put in an appearance at the Geneva Show and elsewhere, but it would not go on sale until later in the year.

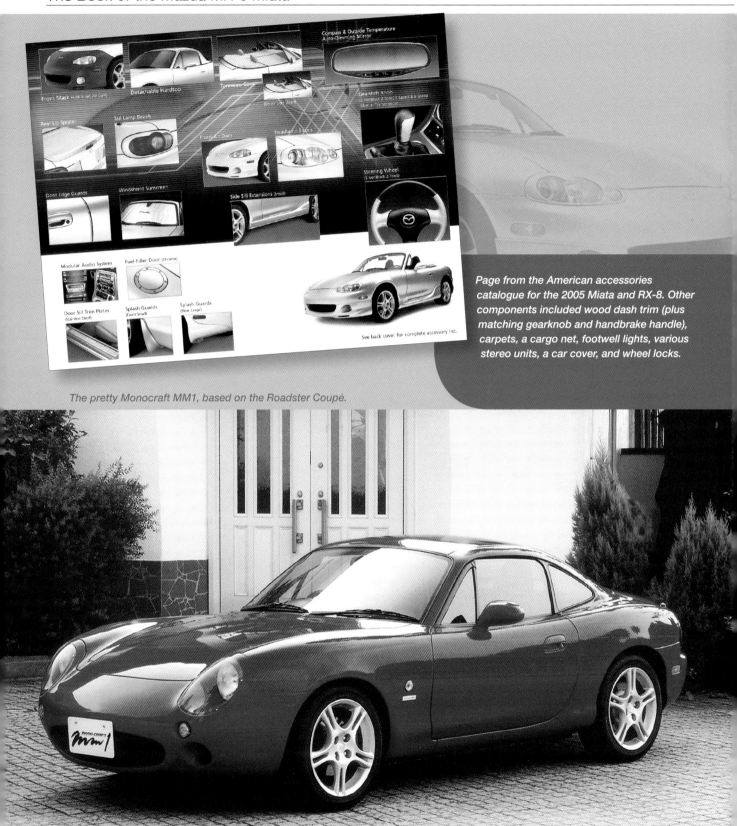

Compass & Outside Temperature
Auto-Dimming Mirror

Front Mask (with Front Air Dam) Detachable Hardtop Tonneau Cover (Driver Side Show) Gearshift Knob (Silver/Black 2-Tone) 5 Speed & 6 Speed Manual Transmission

Rear Lip Spoiler Tail Lamp Bezels Front Air Dam Headlamp Bezels

Steering Wheel (Silver/Black 2-Tone)

Door Edge Guards Windshield Sunscreen Side Sill Extensions (Small)

Modular Audio System Fuel-Filler Door (Chrome)

Door Sill Trim Plates (Stainless Steel) Splash Guards (Front Small) Splash Guards (Rear Large)

See back cover for complete accessory list.

Page from the American accessories catalogue for the 2005 Miata and RX-8. Other components included wood dash trim (plus matching gearknob and handbrake handle), carpets, a cargo net, footwell lights, various stereo units, a car cover, and wheel locks.

The pretty Monocraft MM1, based on the Roadster Coupé.

After the UK, Germany provided Mazda with its biggest MX-5 market in Europe. BMW probably started the 'Art Car' movement, but as this picture shows, German artists are quick to adapt.

The Roadster Coupé Circuit Trial shown at the 2005 Tokyo Auto Salon actually made its debut at the 2004 Auto Salon as the TS Concept, when it was finished in red, with white wheels and a black interior.

Regulations booklet for the 2005 Party Race series, a one-make series aimed at Mazda Roadster and RX-8 owners. As in previous years, it was held over four rounds on some of Japan's top circuits.

Just before Christmas 2004, the author received an e-mail from Tom Matano saying that Disney/Pixar was working on a film called *Cars*, (continued on page 136) and the Miata would have a starring role! Incidentally, having retired from Mazda, Matano is now a lecturer in California, a state where he feels relaxed and at home, surrounded by nice cars and with the sun on his back.

In the UK, by far the biggest MX-5 market in Europe, the 2005 model year line-up was much the same. The 1.6i was priced at £15,000, with the 1.8i at £15,500, and the flagship Sport at £18,000.

Mazda UK couldn't resist one final special edition – the MX-5 Icon, which was announced on 25 March 2005. Priced at £16,600 in 1.6i guise, or £17,100 for the 1.8i version, the Icon came with 15-inch five-spoke alloys, a cloth top, foglights, heated black leather seats, a black leather steering wheel, gearknob and handbrake lever (all with orange stitching), stainless treadplates, windblocker, CD player, remote central locking, and a voucher for up to £500 worth of accessories to personalize each car.

Four body colours were available – two new (Chilli Orange Mica and Black Mica) and two familiar shades, namely Titanium Grey and Sunlight Silver.

End of one era, start of another ...

Production of the NB2 model actually ended in December 2004, so any sales made after this date were furnished from existing stock. Indeed, when the author's wife ordered her car, the exact model she wanted was no longer available, and it was more a question of finding out what was still in Hiroshima rather than picking a specification from the catalogue. But at least the run-out was successful, allowing the new car to come online without a massive stockpile of second generation vehicles left in a corner of a parking lot gathering dust.

Interestingly, while the Mazda truck business was assigned to Isuzu in 2003, a Chinese plant was opened in 2005, but it's doubtful it will have any influence on Mazda's sports car production. For the foreseeable future, the MX-5 and RX-8 would (thankfully) continue to be built in Hiroshima, the place of their birth, thus ensuring their character remained fully intact.

Retaining the character of the MX-5 was a key development area for Takao Kijima and his team during the birth of the third generation Roadster, and it is that story that we take up in the next volume ...

APPENDIX

NB-series production figures

The calendar year figures below are taken from official Mazda records. The table shows production figures (including prototypes in 1997) and the number of cars exported in each year, along with running totals for each. NB production ended in December 2004.

Year	Production	Cumulative totals	Exports	Cumulative exports
1997	2457	2457	0	0
1998	58,682	61,139	48,352	48,352
1999	44,851	105,990	41,380	89,732
2000	47,496	153,486	41,674	131,406
2001	38,870	192,356	35,460	166,866
2002	40,754	233,110	37,586	204,452
2003	30,106	263,216	29,054	233,506
2004	24,232	287,448	23,153	256,659

Total number of NB series models produced **287,448 units**
Total number of NB series models exported **256,659 units**

Note: For reference and comparison, a total of 431,506 NA-series vehicles were built, of which 312,969 were exported.

This second table breaks down NB-series sales in the main markets, including Japan, the USA, Canada, Europe (which includes the UK) and Australia.

Year	Japanese sales	American sales	Canadian sales	European sales	Australian sales
1998	10,166	18,469	1047	16,831	1310
1999	4952	17,738	1198	21,128	1354
2000	4644	18,299	1328	19,264	1038
2001	4211	16,486	1271	16,366	924
2002	2934	14,392	1230	19,663	698
2003	1520	10,920	1079	18,931	540
2004	1646	9356	1146	13,900	483
Totals	**30,073**	**105,660**	**8299**	**126,083**	**6347**

Note: The 1998 figures for Japan and the US have been corrected to cover NB-series cars only, while those for other countries may include a handful of NA models. Likewise, there could be a few NBs sold in 2005, albeit a small number again; the vast majority of 2005 sales will be NC models, so these will be included in a later book.

Interestingly, the US accounted for almost half of NA production, but Stateside demand dropped off for the NB (as it did in Japan, to an even greater extent), while those in the European market warmed to the NB, almost doubling their sales compared to the figures for the NA-series run.

GET
LOST ...

k, from Veloce!

Definitive history of the first generation Mazda MX-5 – also known as the Miata or Eunos Roadster. A fully revised version of an old favourite, now focussing on the original NA series, this book covers all major markets, and includes stunning contemporary photography gathered from all over the world.

ISBN: 978-1-845847-78-4
Hardback • 25x20.7cm • 144 pages
• 221 pictures

The complete history of Mazda's rotary engine-powered vehicles, from Cosmo 110S to RX-8. Charting the challenges, sporting triumphs, and critical reactions to a new wave of sports sedans, wagons, sports cars ... and trucks!

ISBN: 978-1-845849-43-6
Hardback • 25x20.7cm • 192 pages
• 233 colour pictures

Having this book in your pocket is just like having a marque expert by your side. Benefit from the author's years of real ownership experience, learn how to spot a bad car quickly, and how to assess a promising one like a true professional. Get the right car at the right price!

ISBN: 978-1-845842-31-4
Paperback • 19.5x13.9cm • 64 pages
• 107 colour pictures

email: **info@veloce.co.uk** Tel: **+44(0)1305 260068**

Veloce SpeedPro books –

978-1-903706-59-6

978-1-903706-75-6

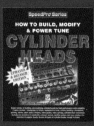
978-1-903706-76-3

978-1-903706-99-2

978-1-845840-21-1

978-1-787111-68-4

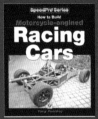
978-1-787111-69-1

978-1-787111-73-8

978-1-845841-87-4

978-1-845842-07-9

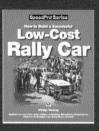
978-1-845842-08-6

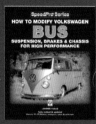
978-1-845842-62-8

978-1-845842-89-5

978-1-845842-97-0

978-1-845843-15-1

978-1-845843-55-7

978-1-845844-33-2

978-1-845844-38-7

978-1-845844-83-7

978-1-845846-15-2

978-1-845848-33-0

978-1-787111-76-9

978-1-845848-69-9

978-1-845849-60-3

978-1-845840-19-8

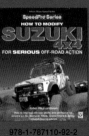
978-1-787110-92-2

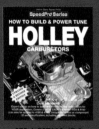
978-1-787110-47-2

978-1-903706-94-7

978-1-787110-87-8

978-1-787111-79-0

978-1-787110-01-4

978-1-901295-26-9

978-1-845844-14-1

978-1-787110-91-5

978-1-787110-88-5

978-1-903706-78-7